TRUMP 2.5

Also by Taufiq Rahim
Middle East in Crisis & Conflict: A Primer

TAUFIQ RAHIM

TRUMP 2.5

A PRIMER

2040 WORLD

Trump 2.5: A Primer
© 2025, Taufiq Rahim. All rights reserved.

Published by 2040 World, New York, N.Y. 10001

ISBN: 979-8-9901347-2-0 (paperback)
ISBN: 979-8-9901347-3-7 (eBook)
Library of Congress Control Number: 2025905845

Publisher's Cataloging-in-Publication
(Provided by Cassidy Cataloguing Services, Inc.)
Names: Rahim, Taufiq, author.
Title: Trump 2.5 : a primer / Taufiq Rahim.
Other titles: Trump two-point-five
Description: New York, N.Y : 2040 World, [2025] | Includes bibliographical references.
Identifiers: LCCN: 2025905845 | ISBN: 9798990134720 (paperback) | 9798990134737 (ebook)
Subjects: LCSH: Trump, Donald, 1946- | Presidents--United States--Biography. | United States--Politics and government--21st century. | LCGFT: Biographies. | BISAC: POLITICAL SCIENCE / American Government / Executive Branch. | BIOGRAPHY & AUTOBIOGRAPHY / Presidents & Heads of State. | HISTORY / United States / 21st Century.
Classification: LCC: E913 .R34 2025 | DCC: 973.933092--dc23

No part of this publication may be reproduced or used in any manner without the prior written permission of the copyright owner, except for fair use.

Although the publisher and the author have made every effort to ensure that the information in this book was correct at the time of publication, and while this publication is designed to provide accurate information regarding the subject matter covered, the publisher, and the author assume no responsibility for errors, inaccuracies, omissions, or any other inconsistencies herein and hereby disclaim any liability to any party for any loss, damage, or disruption caused by errors or omissions, whether such errors or omissions result from negligence, accident, or any other cause.

To request additional permissions or for general inquiries, contact print@2040.world

CONTENTS

PREFACE i

   I UP FRONT 1

  II THE MAN, THE MYTH, AND MAGA 13

 III PRINCIPLES AND POLICIES 47

 IV PEOPLE AND POSITIONS 93

  V THE WAY FORWARD 155

ADDITIONAL RESOURCES 177

PREFACE

The return of Donald Trump to the American presidency was a shock but not necessarily a surprise. In the eyes of many observers, he had been relegated to history after the events of January 6, 2021. Trump's victory on November 5, 2024, exposed that many establishment institutions still lacked a proper understanding of him and the movement he leads.

This publication provides a structured overview at the outset of President Trump's second term. It is not intended to be political or determine whether specific policies are right or wrong. Instead, it takes a clear-eyed view in hopes that well-informed individuals and institutions will be able to engage constructively. By doing so, they can achieve outcomes that benefit America and the world.

Trying to understand, document, and synthesize the agenda of the new American administration is a challenge. The very nature of President Trump makes this effort a moving target. Distilling an actual policy from a more notional statement to move the goalposts in a negotiation is a distinct challenge. Yet, that is what the following chapters set out to do.

Given the numerous executive orders, policy statements, legal documents, and other reporting on record, this primer is not meant to be a library of open-source material. Instead, it seeks to capture what is outlined elsewhere and convey it in an accessible frame for observers. The appendix includes additional resources where interested readers can find facts and figures alluded to in the rest of the text.

This edition was updated on April 1, 2025. Given the speed and intensity to ensure publication, there may be limited missteps in dates, titles, formal names, and minor details. Where possible, new information will be included on the official website, TrumpPrimer.com. In addition, in light of the fast-moving situation, readers will need to incorporate the latest news and developments into their understanding of the administration.

I
UP FRONT

On January 20, 2025, President Donald J. Trump was inaugurated as the 47th president of the United States. It was a remarkable comeback for a political figure who was in the crosshairs of those who opposed him. Following his first term, Trump faced successive criminal investigations, partly due to the events of January 6, 2021. Then, on July 13, 2024, an assassination attempt almost took his life. Another attempt, on September 15, 2024, raised the tensions further. Fate seemed to be thwarting the former president's return to office.

As a private citizen, Trump considered entering the political scene in the 1980s. In the 2000s, he was more serious in this effort, exploring what political party affiliation would be most appropriate. He chose to pursue, at least for a time, the leadership of the Reform Party. Ahead of the 2012 U.S. presidential election, Trump made overtures about seeking the Republican Party nomination.

At the time, Trump was still considered a fringe figure in political circles. His public prominence centered on hosting the show *The Apprentice*. During the 2011 White House Correspondents' Association (WHCA) dinner, then-President Barack Obama directly attacked Trump, mocking his political aspirations. It never occurred to the

Democratic Party, the mainstream media, or establishment institutions to take Trump seriously as a political rival.

On June 16, 2015, Trump, with wife Melania by his side, descended the escalators in Trump Tower in New York to formally announce that he would pursue the Republican nomination for president. His dramatic speech, with its sharp rhetoric, immediately ruffled feathers. The subsequent campaign upended the nature of politics, attacking core party positions that previously had been considered off-limits.

Trump was an underdog, and his chances of victory were discounted in the press. The odds of him ascending to the presidency were seen as impossibly slim by most politicians on both the left and right. But something happened, first gradually and then suddenly. In the Republican debates, Trump began to take down his rivals one by one. In the overall presidential race, against a formidable opponent on the Democratic side, his chances were discounted once again. When he was declared the winner on election night, despite the past controversies laid bare, there were audible gasps in America's newsrooms.

As Trump assumed the presidency on January 20, 2017, *The New York Times*, *The Washington Post*, and other publications characterized him as an illegitimate president. The ongoing intrigue about links with Russia encouraged this viewpoint. A few Trump administration officials were also under suspicion for alleged links to foreign governments. Midway through his presidency, an impeachment proceeding related to Ukraine dominated headlines.

While his first term was chaotic and not without controversy, Trump made serious domestic and foreign policy changes that have had lasting implications. These included the Abraham Accords in the Middle East, the imposition of tariffs on China, and the promotion of domestic manufacturing, among other examples.

Ultimately, the pandemic proved too much for the president and the country to absorb. His popularity flagged, creating an opening ahead of the 2020 election. Joe Biden, Obama's vice president, challenged and defeated Trump, riding the back of an unprecedented mail-in vote to dislodge the incumbent president. In 2016, Trump won the Electoral College 306 to 232 by unexpectedly winning the 'blue wall' states of Pennsylvania, Michigan, and Wisconsin. Biden reversed those gains in 2020, as well as Trump's Electoral College numbers from the previous cycle.

On January 6, 2021, thousands of protestors who had descended on Washington, DC, to contest the election headed toward the U.S. Capitol. The subsequent events saw protestors brazenly marching through the Capitol building, onto the House floor, and into the Speaker's office.

These scenes, including congresspersons kneeling underneath tables for cover, led to swift action. The vandalism that resulted shocked politicians across both sides of the aisle. While Donald Trump called on his supporters to be peaceful before, during, and after these events, his rhetoric maintained that fraud had been perpetrated on the American people and that the election had been stolen.

Many senators and members of Congress were quick to condemn the president, although some refrained from joining the chorus. President Trump was impeached by the House but not convicted by the Senate. Still reeling from the election outcome, Trump refused to attend President Joe Biden's inauguration.

After the departure of the 45th president from office, epitaphs were quickly written about his political career. While by 2024, Trump's re-election may have seemed probable, when he left office in 2021, the deck was stacked against him. It was not just the media and establishment institutions that resisted his return. Numerous legal cases emerged that kept the former president mired in the courts.

Nevertheless, by election day on November 5, 2024, Trump was as popular as ever. Each legal case had strengthened him in the eyes of his base, and the assassination attempts only added to his lore. The events of January 6, 2021, did not resonate while other issues took precedence for voters. His victory in 2024 was definitive, and today, Donald Trump is seen as the legitimate president of the United States, elected with the popular support of the American people.

Election Results

Donald Trump received 77,302,580 votes to 75,017,613 for Kamala Harris. The Electoral College tally was 312 votes for Trump against 226 for Harris. He won all seven proverbial swing states: Pennsylvania, Michigan, Wisconsin, Nevada, North Carolina, Georgia, and Arizona.

The outcome was decisive, even if it was close, as in most recent presidential elections. In 90% of counties in the United States, Trump's vote share increased compared to 2020. He received 15 million more votes in 2024 than he did in 2016.

In the Senate, four seats flipped for the Republicans: Pennsylvania (Sen. Dave McCormick), Montana (Sen. Tim Sheehy), Ohio (Sen. Bernie Moreno), and West Virginia (Sen. Jim Justice). However, the Democrats held the line in four states where Trump won the electoral vote: Michigan (Sen. Elissa Slotkin), Wisconsin (Sen. Tammy Baldwin), Nevada (Sen. Jacky Rosen), and Arizona (Sen. Ruben Gallego). The final Senate tally was 53 Republicans to 47 Democrats, which includes two independents who caucus with the Democrats.

The 2024 elections also produced a Republican majority in the House. The count was 220 for the Republicans and 215 for the Democrats. This was close to the 2022 election outcome but reflected an underperformance in House races, particularly in New York and California. In that sense, the Republican Party polled behind the top of the ticket, losing two seats.

Vibe Shift

The election also demonstrated a deeper vibe shift. Certain minority groups and younger voters broke for Trump, upending the consensus on what constituted a Democratic coalition. A sizable share of Latino men, Arab Americans, and Native Americans voted for Trump over Harris. Trump gained ground across most groups and demographics, with the highest increase among Generation Z (Gen Z) men.

Given the diverse representation, the composition of this voting bloc provides President Trump and his allies with partial insulation against accusations of racism. Separately, the Democratic Party's rubric of a 'rainbow' coalition is called into question. Even lower-income voters swung for the Republican candidate for the first time in decades, another blow to the Democrats.

Yet the vibe shift is more far-reaching, a cultural phenomenon rather than just a political one. The Trump campaign made two significant inroads in the election cycle. One was into Silicon Valley, a traditional Democratic stronghold as high-profile technologists endorsed the Republican candidate in the summer of 2024. The other move was building affinity with younger voters through engagement with podcast hosts and streamers, giving the campaign a coolness factor that the GOP did not have before.

Early Developments

On January 20, 2025, Donald Trump was inaugurated as the 47th president. Despite the fact that the main swearing-in was moved indoors, tens of thousands of supporters flooded Washington, DC. In his Inaugural Address, he called January 20, 2025, "Liberation Day" and, after some rhetorical flourishes, listed policies he would enact, with an emphasis on the border.

He also highlighted newer ideas. These included establishing an External Revenue Service (ERS) to collect tariff revenue, proposing to rename the Gulf of Mexico the Gulf of America, and suggesting that America would "take back" the Panama Canal.

On day one he signed over two dozen executive orders. They covered a range of domestic and foreign policy issues linked to core campaign promises. Notable ones included: "Ending Radical and Wasteful Government DEI Programs and Preferencing," "Unleashing American Energy," "Withdrawing the United States from the World Health Organization," "Establishing and Implementing the President's 'Department of Government Efficiency,'" and "Protecting the American People Against Invasion."

World leaders congratulated Trump on his victory almost immediately after the election and began to engage with him before he assumed the presidency. To a great extent, the Trump administration has been underway since early November 2024, which is why he and his team were able to hit the ground running at such a rapid pace.

Inauguration week also showcased another aspect that enabled the Trump administration to move quickly. A vibrant coalition—the heads of America's business community, top-ranked podcasters, and, in a break with precedent, several world leaders—was present. They attended formal events at the Capitol Rotunda and noteworthy balls and parties around town.

The initial weeks of the administration saw dramatic moves on the domestic front and in foreign affairs. The White House took a multifaceted approach to enacting its early agenda. One of the more surprising developments was the formal nature of the newly established Department of Government Efficiency (DOGE), which now functions as the tip of the spear across the federal bureaucracy.

Domestically, the administration has removed anything related to diversity, equity, and inclusion (DEI) throughout the government. It has also emphasized the border, where there has been a reduction in illegal entries by over 90% since Trump took office for his second term. It has moved to defund and dismantle government bodies, such as USAID and potentially the Department of Education. These moves have been contested in the courts.

The Trump administration dispatched envoys to negotiate and address the Middle East and Ukraine conflicts. This has led to intermittent developments, and the jury is still out as to how sustainable they are. There has also been an emphasis on bringing American prisoners held abroad back home. The threat of tariffs—and, in some cases, their enactment—has led to tension with U.S. neighbors Mexico and Canada, and threats of retaliation from around the world.

President Trump has been pushing the envelope in the early days, even by his standards. His proposals that Canada could become the 51st state and that Gaza would similarly come under American ownership engendered an outlandish feeling from the outset. What should be taken seriously and what is bluster? In that sense, conventional rules are truly falling by the wayside, even by the benchmark of Trump's first term.

What to Pay Attention to

Now that the administration is underway and most personnel have been appointed and, where required, confirmed, the key will be to see how quickly the White House moves forward. Since 2026 is an election year, there is a narrow window to demonstrate progress. While the executive branch can drive the agenda, meaningful changes require alignment with Congress, and this is likely to be a continuing challenge.

While the Republicans have a majority in the Senate, a few Republican senators are lukewarm to the Make America Great Again (MAGA) movement. More partisan changes will be tough to push through the Senate. The majority in the House is also razor-thin due in part to the nomination of representatives to cabinet positions. Three defections or abstentions on a vote could potentially undermine the Republican side.

The other challenge is already coming from the judiciary. As in the first Trump term, there have been constant judicial reviews of executive orders. Even the Biden administration was thwarted at times by the courts, as in the case of cancellation of student debt.

Judicial objections to the Trump administration's policies will continue given the president's many executive orders. The courts will also evaluate any modification of government bodies that fall under legislation passed by Congress. The frequency of these rulings and how quickly they are resolved will affect the momentum of the president's agenda.

Most existing legal cases against Trump personally have been dismissed at the federal level. Additional legal targeting by federal investigators—which was aggressive during the first Trump administration, ensnaring Mike Flynn, Paul Manafort, and others—will not be as involved this time. In addition, impeachment in Congress will be much harder to materialize. There is also no ongoing investigation, as there was during Trump's first term, which led to the appointment of a special counsel early on.

Potential investigations and legal cases launched by individual states, however, are on the horizon. These do not need to be against Trump himself but could target multiple members of his circle or administration. This could become a growing hindrance.

Trump officials have already begun to 'clean up' the Department of Justice (DOJ) and law enforcement agencies, motivated by distrust stemming from the legal challenges

President Trump faced when he was out of office. This is being replicated in other bureaucratic arms of the government. There is likely to be continuous pushback and confrontation between elements of the bureaucracy and the administration as this develops.

These confrontations could undermine progress and spill over into the halls of Congress. They could also provide breathing room to enable a consolidated opposition to new policies. Nevertheless, the Democrats do not have unified leadership, and fewer Republicans are willing to join them openly in attacking President Trump or his policies.

On the economic front, abrupt policy shifts will sometimes undermine the markets. The economy was preliminarily buoyed in 2025 by federal reserve decisions, proposed tax cuts, energy and corporate deregulation, and indications of growth. However, the administration's policies, notably its tariff-first position, could lead to sustained headwinds. As markets move, short-term pain and interim price spikes could arise. These could undermine the administration's approval ratings and lead to public discontent, reinforcing pushback on the administration, even in Republican circles.

The first year may also see challenges to the White House from abroad. China, Russia, Iran, and North Korea will try to determine where the red lines are for the new Trump administration. In addition, Trump will pursue so-called grand bargains, and there will be a desire to shore up starting positions from which to negotiate. As with all geopolitical flashpoints and rivalries, there will be intended and unintended consequences. The extent of this volatility could distract the White House from its priorities as it puts out fires globally while President Trump alternatingly engages in social media diplomacy and conflict with geopolitical foes.

How to Get Information

Almost all political media and analyses come with bias. In addition, so-called 'independent' voices are not necessarily more objective than the mainstream press, as they are often motivated to drive engagement through clickbait. This reinforces the promotion of stories driven by shock value to play to their audiences' baser instincts.

The ability to discern fact from fiction is becoming extremely difficult. The hype cycle involves multiple accounts echoing the same story so that it appears singularly powerful, even if the underlying sourcing is thin. Without investigating beyond the headlines, the audience risks missing more significant developments and context.

Each individual curates the news differently and, depending on their needs, will require a unique approach and set of sources. There is too much content, and while consuming a great deal of it may seem necessary, that consumption often does not sway the overall picture. The 24-hour binge cycle has rapidly diminishing returns when it comes to being informed. For those seeking to track developments, combining a mix of specialized inputs, including news media, social media, and in-person engagement, is best.

As new developments come to light, it will be important to have a stable roster of sources, including those mentioned in the appendix of this book and on the official website TrumpPrimer.com.

How to Read This Primer

The first year of the new Trump administration will unquestionably be full of volatility, noise, and jockeying for positions from all sides. This primer draws a framework for understanding the administration's agenda. There are five chapters, each providing a dimension of understanding. Some are more detailed and information-filled, while others are more expository. They can be read independently or sequentially.

This first chapter, "Up Front," lays the groundwork for the current moment and charts early developments.

The second chapter, "The Man, the Myth, and MAGA," delves into Donald Trump's background, origin story, and political evolution.

The third chapter, "Principles and Policies," outlines the Trump administration's underlying philosophy and perspectives on issues, which form the foundation of its governance.

The fourth chapter, "People and Positions," provides an organized list of key personnel across the administration. This is the densest section and might be best considered as an index to refer back to.

The final chapter, "The Way Forward," examines potential moments over the next four years and suggests how best to engage with them.

The appendix, "Additional Resources," contains a wide range of sources that can help readers better understand the president and his movement.

Every day will assuredly bring 'new' news. What is a headline today may fall to the back page tomorrow. Yet, through it all, the themes remain the same. And they all fall under the banner of Trump 2.5.

II

THE MAN, THE MYTH, AND MAGA

Donald John Trump is arguably the most well-known and powerful person on the planet today. This may be hard to fathom for a figure considered a celebrity and showman for much of his life.

Yet, today, President Trump presides over one of the most expansive political forces—the United States of America—the world has ever seen. In recent decades, the presidency has often been derided as a symbolic office in the sense that no individual has ultimate control, given the term limits and the institutional fabric of the government. Trump, however, is expanding the breadth of executive power with each passing day. Federal courts are already testing the limits of this.

In winning a second term, Trump had to defeat his political opponents and all other obstacles in his path. Regardless of whether the opposition to him was correct and whether his victory was a good or bad thing, there is no question that it was a remarkable triumph. His ability to succeed demonstrates the strength of his political operation and his movement's financial, political, and legal depth.

Like any political leader, President Trump is partly beholden to behind-the-scenes interests, both visible and invisible. While he is independently wealthy today, select individuals have been financially instrumental in his campaign and business dealings. Whether President Trump governs independently or in concert with those interests will become apparent as his second term progresses.

Regardless, President Trump entered office attempting to be the most empowered president in American history since Franklin D. Roosevelt, who shaped modern America—and the world. In its first executive orders, the Trump administration looked to remove obstacles in the bureaucracy that could block the implementation of the president's writ. With his online movement and financial backers—including the wealthiest individual on Earth, Elon Musk—the power is immense.

How did all of this come to pass? What motivates Donald Trump? How does he see himself and his life? How might that inform the ways in which his second term will unfold?

The Man

Before Donald Trump emerged as a businessman, a celebrity, and ultimately a politician, he was a young boy growing up under his father's mentorship in one of the most vibrant cities in the world during its definitive rise. His family and these formative years forged his personality, temperament, and outlook. Depicted often as a caricature, it is easy to forget that Trump is a man with all the same emotions and feelings as others. Understanding him in this context and through his life experience is vital to understanding the depth of his current stances.

Early Years to Later Life

Donald John Trump was born June 14, 1946, in the New York City borough of Queens, to Fred and Mary Trump. His father was a well-known real estate developer who concentrated on the outer boroughs. Fred Trump died in 1999, and Mary Trump passed away just a year later. Both parents had a heavy influence on Donald Trump, who was the fourth of five siblings.

According to reports, he has remained close to his immediate family throughout the years. His oldest sister, Maryanne Trump Barry, became a federal judge and passed away in 2023; while never publicly critical of Donald, she may have had private misgivings. His younger brother, Robert Trump, was like a close friend and passed away in 2020. His other sister, Elizabeth Trump Grau, continues to support him and attended his inauguration.

The individual who impacted him most was his older brother, Fred Trump Jr. When he died in 1981 at 42, it left an indelible mark on the younger Donald. During his lifetime, Fred Jr. eschewed the family business, became a pilot, and battled alcoholism. Ultimately, he lost this fight and died as a result.

The death of Fred Jr. catalyzed a sense of urgency in Donald Trump and inspired a practice of discipline. The word 'discipline' might not come to mind for most readers regarding Trump. Maybe 'excess' would be more appropriate. Fred Jr. regularly cautioned Donald against both drinking and smoking, citing his own experience as a cautionary tale. As a consequence, Donald Trump has avoided smoking and drinking throughout his life.

Today, the president is seen conducting toasts with world leaders with Diet Coke filling his cup. Trump subsequently instructed his children to avoid drinking, smoking, and drugs, although they may not have followed his advice. This lifestyle perhaps has helped Trump maintain the stamina needed to work demanding hours with relentless energy well into his 70s. Certainly, it is not attributable to his famous McDonald's diet, which he imbibes almost daily. Outside of playing golf, he is not known to exercise vigorously.

Having remained close to his parents and siblings throughout his life, Donald Trump has also kept his children close to him despite two divorces. He married model Ivana Zelníčková in 1977, at the age of 30. Together, they had three children—Donald Trump Jr., Eric Trump, and Ivanka Trump. The marriage ended in 1990, and he subsequently married Marla Maples, another model with whom it was rumored he had an earlier affair.

Trump's marriage to Maples, which produced a daughter, Tiffany Trump, ended in 1999. In 2005, he married model Melania Knavs, and they have remained together since. They have one son, Barron Trump, who is currently a student at New York University. Since their marriage, Melania Trump has focused on family, with forays into business, fashion, and philanthropy.

Trump has remained close to his five children and 10 grandchildren. His youngest daughter, Tiffany, is expecting her first child, so that number will soon grow. His children have been involved in his business and political life to varying degrees. To a great extent, Trump's family is his organization, and vice versa.

While Trump is a New Yorker who returned to the city after obtaining his bachelor's degree from the Wharton School of Business at the University of Pennsylvania, in recent years, he has been equally at home, if not more so, at his Florida estate of Mar-a-Lago. The property was acquired in 1985 and converted over time into a private members' club and a personal residence for Trump.

Mar-a-Lago was built by heiress Marjorie Merriweather Post, who aspired to convert it into a so-called 'Winter White House.' Upon her death, she gifted the estate to the U.S. government for that purpose, but it was never used as such. President Jimmy Carter restored the property to private hands, and it was subsequently sold to Trump.

Following his first term, President Trump formally moved his residence to Florida for business reasons and after becoming increasingly unpopular in his hometown of New York City. It was quite an about-turn for Trump, who was not only a fixture in Manhattan but had also built some of its iconic buildings there, including Trump Tower on Fifth Avenue, where he maintains a home in the penthouse.

While the Trump Organization, the vehicle for his holdings, still has a significant presence in New York, Trump spends his time when not at the White House at either Mar-a-Lago or his golf courses, notably the Bedminster Club in New Jersey. Yet, the allure of New York has never truly gone away for Trump.

The Family Business

When Trump was given the reins of the family business, he ventured from Queens to Manhattan to become a builder, much to his father's chagrin. It is no surprise that Trump held a flagship rally in 2024 at Madison Square Garden in New York, a state he was never due to win, but in a city that still has tremendous emotional appeal for him to this day.

Trump's detractors will point to his father, who gave him a hefty allowance in his early days, as the source of his business power. This viewpoint maintains that Trump inherited his wealth and has alternatively squandered it or benefitted from appreciating property values. The events of the early 1990s, when Trump straddled the line with bankruptcy, certainly add to this perspective; several of his properties in Atlantic City went insolvent around that time.

The truth of his wealth and inheritance is between his claims and those of his detractors. Indeed, he started out with his father's financial support and business connections. Concerning his inheritance, media estimates have ranged from $20 million to $400 million. While there are no definitive reports, he is worth over $5 billion today, and even at his recent low point after his presidency, his net worth was still estimated to be at least $2.5 billion.

The jury will always be out on the extent of Trump's business empire and whether he deserves any accolades. Yet, after he took hold of the family business, he emerged as a successful real estate developer in the city known for its skyscrapers. After his dip in the 1990s, he came back to build an even larger business footprint.

Real Estate

Trump entered the real estate scene in the mid-1970s. As an audacious 28-year-old, he offered to buy the soon-to-be boarded-up Commodore Hotel, which he eventually acquired and relaunched as the Grand Hyatt Hotel. That building put Trump on the map in his own right. The success of that development was based on his ability to bring together diverse stakeholders for approvals in New York's nebulous regulatory and political landscape.

The next significant milestone for the Trump Organization was the Trump Tower on Fifth Avenue. This project, too, involved complex negotiations. Trump bought the airspace above the adjacent flagship Tiffany Store to prevent another building from blocking the view from the tower's residences and for other zoning reasons. When it launched in 1983, Trump Tower was a dramatic addition to the city, which was on an economic upswing in the 1980s.

Within months of opening the tower for sales, prices rocketed. The average price of an apartment in 1983 was $1 million, equivalent to about $3 million in today's dollars. The building commanded the highest prices per square foot in Manhattan, and its tenants were a who's who of the United States.

Aside from the Fifth Avenue tower, Trump did not necessarily build much of New York's skyline from the ground up. He often acquired and renovated properties, such as 40 Wall Street, with financial backing and co-owners. At other times, he was appointed to lend his name or his organization's sales apparatus to help bring in buyers. The Trump

Organization played a substantial role in developing other notable skyscrapers, such as the Trump World Tower near the United Nations. In addition, Trump had a decades-long involvement in developing what is today known as Riverside Boulevard, which also features Trump Place.

Over the decades, the Trump Organization has worked increasingly on the development of golf courses and the associated property around them. These include the Trump International Golf Club and Trump National Doral in Florida, the Aberdeen and Turnberry courses in Scotland, and of course the Bedminster Club in New Jersey. The latter was the first course developed end-to-end by Trump's team.

Today, there are about 10 hotels, 20 golf courses, nearly 40 residential properties (operating or under development), and assorted commercial developments and private estates in the portfolio. Overall, it is hard to discern the extent of Trump's and the Trump Organization's ownership in the properties bearing his name. In addition, over the years, he became known as much for managing properties as for developing them.

Media and Entertainment
In the late 1980s and 1990s, Trump was also involved in the entertainment sector. He owned and operated the Miss Universe Organization for two decades. He also led engagements in sports promotion, notably boxing. This foray into the entertainment business contributed to his lore, wealth, and network.

Interestingly, much of Trump's work in media related to Atlantic City, which became a hosting ground for marquee events. It was there in 2001 when he partnered with Dana White to host the Ultimate Fighting Championship (UFC). That led to a lifelong relationship that helped him develop popularity with Gen Z males and the podcaster Joe Rogan.

The Apprentice television show markedly increased Trump's earnings in the 2000s. It also cemented a relationship with producer Mark Burnett, considered one of the biggest names in the television industry throughout the 2000s and 2010s. In December 2024, Trump appointed Burnett as a Special Envoy to the United Kingdom.

Heading into the 2016 presidential election, Trump's business holdings were primarily a mix of urban real estate, golf courses and resorts, and entertainment assets. In 2021, after leaving office, Trump entered a new space and launched a digital media company, Trump Media & Technology Group (TMTG), helmed by former Congressman Devin Nunes. This company houses the social media platform Truth Social and is publicly traded after a merger with a special purpose acquisition company in 2024.

More recently, members of the Trump family helped create World Liberty Financial to operate in decentralized finance. Under this umbrella, the $Trump meme coin was launched just ahead of Trump's inauguration. It is another indication that although Trump is focused on the presidency, he will continue to profit from his business holdings that leverage his status. His children also have fewer restrictions as they have not joined the administration.

Over the years, and even when he was staving off bankruptcy in the 1990s, Trump's most valuable underlying assets have been his brand and affiliated materials and merchandise. From books to apparel to memorabilia, the Trump Organization has benefitted from the Trump brand, which still has tremendous value as an asset to the business. With Trump's return to the presidency and from social ostracization, the value of this brand will only grow.

Setbacks

Over the decades, Trump has also launched failed enterprises. He has faced numerous lawsuits and accusations of wrongdoing from business partners and consumers. In the 1980s, Trump acquired assets at inflated prices, the Plaza Hotel in New York being one example, which saddled him with rising debt. While his foray into Atlantic City in the late 1980s and early 1990s occurred with much fanfare, it did not have lasting success. The Trump Hotel there was demolished in 2021.

Another setback was the effort to revitalize Eastern Airlines as a luxury-branded service called the Trump Shuttle, which ended in 1992. Other minor forays, such as Trump's engagement with the nascent U.S. Football League in the 1980s, came and went. Later, while building on his profile from *The Apprentice*, he launched Trump University, which only lasted five years and closed in 2010. It prompted several class action lawsuits in subsequent years.

In the early 1990s, amidst business setbacks, Trump faced potential business and personal bankruptcy. Throughout his career, as with other builders, leverage was standard. Yet Trump took it further, often providing personal guarantees that eventually totaled $900 million. This left Trump in a significant loss position by the mid-1990s. In 1991, documents gathered as part of his gaming license review in New Jersey for the Taj Mahal Hotel and Casino indicated that his debt had grown to $3.4 billion, approximately the value of his total assets (and may have been more, depending on valuations).

He came out of that personal and business hole by the decade's end. Partly, this was accomplished through debt restructuring, as lenders did not want to lose the entire value of their loans. Trump also benefitted from rising real estate prices in the 1990s after the 1990-1991 recession. For example, 40 Wall Street was bought by Trump in 1995 for as little as $1.3 million and is today worth north of $200 million. Tax returns, leaked by an employee of the Internal Revenue Service (IRS), showed that he also earned substantial tax credits due to sustained loss positions in his businesses.

Next Generation

As Trump has aged and as he entered politics, his children have taken a more active role in running the Trump Organization. Ivanka Trump, his eldest daughter, was early in the limelight. She graduated from her father's alma mater, Wharton, and became vice president of the Trump Organization. She also became a fashion icon and entrepreneur in her own right. When Ivanka and her husband, Jared Kushner, took on formal positions in the White House, she stepped down from her role in the family business.

Donald Trump Jr. and his brother, Eric Trump, ultimately took on oversight roles in the business during their father's first term. They both serve as executive vice presidents of the company, which may pay homage to the fact that their father is still ultimately at the helm, as there is no listed president.

Over five decades since Trump began his business career in earnest, through all its ups and downs, he remains one of the wealthiest people in America. He has successfully navigated headwinds to consolidate a multifaceted business empire that has a new generation of family leadership.

Controversies and Cover-ups

Over the years, Trump has often been immersed in controversy, so much so that it could be said he courts it. He realized early on that being vilified only increased his prominence. This is how he built his real estate empire, grew his persona on *The Apprentice,* and entered the political stage: playing the villain.

While that persona reflected his personality and theatrics, there were real controversies surrounding Trump in his personal and professional life. These mainly involved allegations of sexual impropriety and racism. In addition, numerous cases were brought over the years in his business dealings, where he was accused of ethical lapses or neglecting the needs of tenants. Trump was almost always in court, either defending against or launching a lawsuit.

It must be said that, in most cases, Trump was able to reach a resolution with claimants. In addition to a steady roster of lawyers to advocate for him, Trump developed a close relationship with New York's top columnists and tabloids over the years. There was a constant stream of stories, often planted by Trump himself throughout the 1980s and 1990s, about him that would feature prominently. They covered everything from his business life to his supposed sexual prowess. Later, with the advent of Twitter (now X), he had a more direct line to the public to build a storyline. He famously targeted Rosie O'Donnell on the platform early in the 2010s.

Many of Trump's moves have detractors to this day. In 1989, he took out a full-page ad calling for the restoration of the death penalty in New York. This came after the confession of the so-called Central Park Five for a brutal crime in the heart of the city. They have since been exonerated.

Most of the claims regarding sexual harassment and impropriety have either been settled or are still being litigated in the courts. Many of these cases came to light after Trump entered politics. The court records are the best source for the latest on them.

Profile and Politics

The notion of Trump as a politician and public figure emerged early, building on his celebrity profile. He appeared on news and talk shows and published books. Gradually, over the years, he began to engage with the political process.

Trump was a master of the television age. His first extended television interview was in 1980 with correspondent Rona Barrett, which can be accessed through the interview database listed in the "Additional Resources" appendix at the end of this book. In that conversation, he spoke to America's "potential" and the idea that the country could go on to regain what it once was so that it "gets the respect of other countries." He also provided a probing reading of the Iranian hostage crisis and the Iran-Iraq war, shedding light on the peace-through-strength inclination that would echo later in his political career. When Barrett asked Trump whether he would ever run for president, he spoke evocatively about the qualities a candidate should embody but stated that he did not desire the role.

In his interview on *The Today Show* with Tom Brokaw in 1980—around the time he launched formal construction on the now-famous Trump Tower—he also limited his political aspirations. A few years later, in an interview on *60 Minutes* in 1985, Mike Wallace pressed him on a number of fronts. In that interview, Trump conveyed a sense of hostility toward the news media. At that point, Trump was becoming more forthright but still refrained from asserting any political ambitions.

By 1987, Trump had intensified his public presence by publishing his book, *The Art of the Deal*. He delved much more deeply into the day's political issues in subsequent media appearances. In an episode of the talk show *Donahue* in December of that year, which highlighted the municipal politics of New York, Trump fully embodied the combative style that he is now known for today. Yet, it was in an interview with Larry King on CNN a few months earlier that Trump's political ambitions on the national stage became apparent. It came shortly after he took out a full-page political ad in major newspapers lambasting American foreign policy.

In that September 1987 ad, Trump pointedly targeted American allies Japan and Saudi Arabia for "taking advantage of the United States" on trade and not paying for the security that America provided. While the countries mentioned may have changed in the four decades since, his stance on the underlying principle has remained unchanged. Trump flirted with running for office in 1987, which he ultimately decided against.

When speaking to Larry King, he claimed he did not want to be president. At the same time, he was outspoken about his positions with King and the show's callers. With one caller from Canada, he even exchanged views on free trade, the reverberations of which have been felt in the beginnings of the current Trump presidency. With another, he spoke about the disproportionate payments made by the U.S. to NATO versus those made by European countries.

Trump attended the Republican National Convention (RNC) in 1988 as a guest of George H.W. Bush, whom he backed. In another interview with Larry King on the floor of the RNC, he claimed to enjoy politics but once again said he had no interest in running. Trump was still fully engaged in the political debates of the time. When appearing on the *Oprah Winfrey Show* that same year, he spoke directly about America's shortcomings and his political stance. He insisted on making allies pay their fair share, as he termed it. In that conversation, as in others, he stated that he would win if he entered the race.

By the late 1980s, Trump was becoming his now-familiar politically combative self as he battled the Democratic establishment in New York and the mayor at the time, Ed Koch. While he built alliances, including with minority communities and activists, among them Jesse Jackson, he did not shy away from positions that put him at odds with societal conventions. When he took out the advertisement calling for capital punishment in the case of the Central Park Five, it alienated newfound political allies.

By 1990, Trump was fading from business prominence, and his political aspirations took a hiatus. It took a decade for his political ambition to re-emerge. However, by that time, Trump, as an outsider, was no longer courted by the Republican Party. In 1997, Trump published *The Art of the*

Comeback, which again brought him into the newsrooms of the day.

Trump's political positions had not changed, but his tactics started to shift. He saw himself having to run the same unorthodox playbook on the political scene as he had in real estate. He would be the outsider and interloper who had to fight the incumbent players. In addition, he would appeal not to the gatekeepers but to the people directly.

In October 1999, Trump formed a preliminary campaign committee to compete for the Reform Party nomination. The 1990s were the age of independent candidates and third parties. This was reinforced following Texas businessman Ross Perot's showing in the 1992 presidential election, in which he obtained roughly 19% of the vote, and former wrestler-turned-politician Jesse Ventura's gubernatorial victory in Minnesota in 1998.

With Republican operative Roger Stone as his campaign manager, Trump took it seriously, appearing on the Sunday talk shows. He also published a book on his platform, *The America We Deserve*, in 2000, which is worth reading today. His main rival at the time was Pat Buchanan, who, ironically, is seen in conservative circles as a precursor to today's Trump.

Trump did not follow through and withdrew from the race in February 2000. Part of the reason for this withdrawal was the chaos of the Reform Party itself. The campaign solidified Trump's name as a potential outsider candidate for future election cycles. It also prodded his return to the Republican Party.

In his 2000 book, Trump highlighted a few issues that subsequent events have reinforced his perspective on. Released before the September 11 attacks, the book covered the rising threat of terrorism. It also spoke of the systemic challenge of China and how the country was getting, as Trump labeled it, an "easy ride."

The book also gave insights into the balancing act that Trump would adopt in later years on social issues. The economic and foreign policy themes remain remarkably similar to today. His platform then—as now—emphasized the importance of respect for America around the world. Immigration was also a topic, but it was not as salient for Trump in 2000 as it would become in later years.

By 2011, several years into his marriage to Melania Trump and with his son, Barron, no longer a toddler, Trump again toyed with the idea of running. Politically, it was a new era. The grassroots of the Republican Party had taken on a nativist tinge in response to Barack Obama's presidency. With the Tea Party movement, there was also pushback against establishment Republicans.

Trump began to increase his political visibility. He expressed his opinions as he always had through New York-based publications and cable news and used a new platform that was rising in prominence: Twitter. At that point, Trump began attacking the incumbent president more directly.

It was surprising but also opportunistic that Trump emerged as a vociferous voice in the so-called birther movement in 2011 that claimed Barack Obama was not born in the United States but instead in Kenya. Trump had placed himself squarely out of the prevailing consensus in political circles. Yet, he also anchored himself as a notable figure in the grassroots of the GOP. Obama even released a version of his birth certificate to silence the noise.

Trump visited battleground states in 2011, with a well-covered stop in New Hampshire. It was the first time he seriously engaged with the Republican primary. He was included in relevant polls and was not so far behind front-runner Mitt Romney, who ultimately won the nomination.

Indeed, hindsight is 20/20, but at the time, following his failure to enter the race and Obama's derisive dismissal at the White House Correspondents' Association dinner in 2011, a Trump presidency seemed a marginal possibility. Perhaps, as critics claimed, he was in it just for publicity.

That, of course, would all change in 2015.

The Myth

As much as there is Trump, the man, Trump has also tried to create a myth around his persona. His rise in business coincided with the buildings he developed and managed at the heart of Manhattan, which symbolized the boom of the 1980s. The value of Trump's enterprises was as much in his name, brand, and mystique as in any physical assets. As long as he symbolized success, more investors wanted to partner with him.

Even when he emerged from the brink of bankruptcy in the mid-1990s, it was a turnaround that left much to the imagination. How had he done a financial Houdini to escape from a seemingly inescapable place? And when he climbed to the top of television ratings, all these intangible elements went into overdrive. The more ubiquitous Trump became, the higher his brand value rose. The higher his brand value rose, the more ubiquitous he became.

Whether the Trump myth was more fiction or fact became irrelevant. He had cemented his recognition in America, and ultimately, this polarizing attachment helped propel him to the highest rung of political power.

What's in a Name

The Trump name became synonymous with a global brand—and more so with an entire concept: wealth. Few people achieved such universal recognition apart from superstar athletes; even fewer had their name become a brand across multiple industry categories. One comparison that comes to mind is Michael Jordan.

It was rare for any one businessman or mogul to have a name synonymous with money and riches in popular culture. During Trump's lifetime, wealthier individuals were everywhere: Steve Jobs, Bill Gates, and Warren Buffett. Trump created a brand from his name and then commodified and monetized it. When he built his iconic building on Fifth Avenue, he called it Trump Tower. Soon after, other Trump properties followed. At one point, he even had a line of branded Trump Steaks. Decades later, developers today still pay to borrow the Trump name to place on their towers, hotels, and estates.

The Trump name became synonymous in the 1980s, 1990s, and well into the 2000s with wealth to such a degree that it was used in numerous hip-hop songs to that effect, including by the Beastie Boys, Ice Cube, Master P, Kid Rock, Jay-Z, Nelly, Ludacris, and A Tribe Called Quest, to name a few. Beyond wealth, Trump became famous for being famous. In many ways, he was the original influencer.

The Zeitgeist

Trump recognized the role of mass media early on. In addition to engaging with the news media and shaping the discourse, he realized that entering the cultural lexicon was just as important. He actively built on his ubiquity and name recognition to do just that in the 1990s and 2000s.

He began a series of television and film appearances just when Americanization was headed into overdrive around the world. He famously appeared in the movies *Home Alone 2*, *Zoolander*, *Two Weeks Notice*, and others. On television, the list includes *The Fresh Prince of Bel-Air*, *The Jeffersons*, and *Sex in the City*.

However, Trump truly entered the cultural zeitgeist in the early 2000s. After the World Trade Center attacks, there was a sense of restoring pride to New York. Trump, being synonymous with buildings, New York, and success, was in a prime position to capture America's attention. Mark Burnett helped Trump do just that with the launch of the hit show *The Apprentice* on NBC.

It is hard to imagine today how pivotal *The Apprentice* was at the time, especially for younger or non-American readers. It was a landmark event when it premiered on January 8, 2004. There was no social media or Facebook, which was founded later in 2004. There was no YouTube, which was founded in 2005. There was no Netflix streaming—that began in 2007. Primetime network television was where America tuned in.

The Apprentice became the most-watched new show on television and was often the most talked-about show. The star was Trump as the boss, decision-maker, and magnate. His catchphrase, "You're fired!" entered the cultural zeitgeist, much as Trump already had. It further catapulted his celebrity so that he had a new reason to be famous in his third decade in the public eye.

Trump etched himself in the minds of a new generation by building on his show *The Apprentice* with *The Celebrity Apprentice* and then used the same persona to engage on other platforms, such as wrestling. His appearance on WWE's *WrestleMania* was iconic. His relationship with NBC led to the opportunity to host *Saturday Night Live*.

The cultural currency that Trump gained during that period added to his persona and his everyman touch. Strangely, despite being a billionaire, quite aloof, and rarely out of a suit, the ubiquity gave people a feeling of being connected to Trump. Yet, through it all, Trump maintained a sense of being above the fray and was not a serious contender for politics and power, despite his intermittent entreaties.

This meant that on the social circuit in New York and Palm Beach, Trump was simply on the invite list, and if he were at a party, it would be talked about. He counted Bill and Hillary Clinton among his friends, and they attended Ivanka Trump's wedding. Ivanka Trump was also a fixture on the social circuit, and many celebrities wore her jewelry, which stopped after she entered the political orbit alongside her father.

Fifth Avenue

This affinity for Trump vanished overnight in many of his familiar circles when he announced his presidential run in 2015. Conversely, for his newfound political fans, the presidential run only deepened his lore. Through his rallies that seemed to double as stand-up routines, his celebrity went to the next level.

It was a strange phenomenon, as the states in which Trump campaigned were not those where he had spent most of his time or where he built his businesses. He did not fit in when in Alabama, Texas, or Tennessee. But he was a big draw immediately, and his supporters became reflexively loyal.

At the beginning of 2016, Trump joked that he could stand in the middle of Fifth Avenue and shoot somebody, and he would not lose any voters. He may not have been wrong. The media missed that Trump was not just a New York figure. He was an American fixture—and had been not just for one year or one decade, but for 40 years by the time he ran for president.

When he did run, he had reached the pinnacle of the business and entertainment worlds and was known by name and as a brand to all generations of Americans. In fact, for many Americans, he represented success more than any other icon. And here he was now, singing their praises and promising to represent their hopes and aspirations. The political potency of that was immense.

MAGA

Make America Great Again rose to prominence as a slogan by Trump and now represents a movement with followers who call themselves "MAGA." That movement has namesake echoes in Make America Healthy Again (MAHA) and Make Europe Great Again (MEGA). The MAGA movement will live past Trump as it has also captured and defined the essence of the Republican Party. How did it all begin?

Escalating Escalators

On June 16, 2015, Donald Trump, with his wife Melania by his side, descended the escalators in Trump Tower in New York to formally announce that he would pursue the Republican nomination for president. His speech immediately created shockwaves. Most themes echoed his general political outlook, which had been relatively consistent over four decades. However, this time, the tone was more strident and direct, if not nasty. In that speech, he claimed that Mexico was sending rapists across the border.

Trump pushed political correctness aside and embraced policy proposals that seemed out of bounds. Early on, he called for a "big, beautiful wall" on the U.S. border with Mexico. He also proposed a so-called 'Muslim ban' and suggested simply taking oil from Iraq. Whether this was hyperbole or bombast, it was clear that the boundaries of acceptable politics were being redrawn.

In the campaign, he made statements and ad hominem attacks on critics that seemed to cross red lines. Regarding one-time Republican presidential candidate John McCain, he famously remarked, "He's a war hero because he was captured. I like people that weren't captured." After a dust-up in one of the debates with Megyn Kelly, who was then at Fox News, he went on to make crude remarks about her menstrual cycle.

Yet, it appeared that nothing could stop Trump from winning the Republican nomination. At the time, Jeb Bush, the former governor of Florida and brother of the last Republican president, George W. Bush, had a formidable war chest and the backing of connected lobbyists. But once on the debate stage next to Trump, Bush's perceived sense of inevitability vanished. Similarly, Senators Ted Cruz and Marco Rubio, and former governors Chris Christie and

Mike Huckabee were no match for Trump. The same was true for all the other candidates. Trump emerged as the last man standing out of 17 contenders.

In the beginning, Trump pursued his political ambitions alone. However, once it became clear he might win the Republican nomination, his primary opponents began to endorse him, even those he had targeted with explicit vitriol. The first was former New Jersey Governor Chris Christie, who was soon followed by renowned surgeon Dr. Ben Carson.

Senator Marco Rubio, whom Trump had nicknamed "Little Marco," endorsed him in June 2016. It took until September for Senator Ted Cruz to endorse Trump, just six weeks before the election. Trump had accused Cruz's father of vague involvement in John F. Kennedy's assassination.

Even after his nomination, there was still palpable opposition to his candidacy in the Senate. Senator Jeff Sessions, a known anti-immigration hawk, was the first Republican senator to endorse Trump, in February 2015. Senate Majority Leader Mitch McConnell offered his endorsement, but only after Trump had secured the Republican primary; it was clear there was a desire to chart an independent GOP course should Trump become president.

The "Never Trump" movement was born around this time. While pundits still discounted his chances to defeat the Democratic front-runner and eventual candidate, Hillary Clinton, this rearguard action to contain his rise was seen as an insurance policy. It comprised well-known Republican leaders, institutions, and publications who coalesced to oppose their party's nominee.

The split within the Republican establishment fostered a perception that support for Trump was limited and that he did not have the real ability to win. Perhaps this led to the shock millions in the country felt when Trump won the election in 2016, as they had been led to believe that this was an impossible scenario. Ahead of the second presidential debate on October 7, 2016, a sensational tape was released of a private conversation between former *Access Hollywood* television host Billy Bush and Trump from a decade earlier, in which he made crude remarks that both his proponents and opponents interpreted as permissive of sexual assault.

After being relegated to second billing in 2008, Clinton's path to the presidency was seemingly inevitable this time around. In many Republican circles, the video was seen as a death knell for Trump's candidacy—so much so that *The Washington Post* ran the headline, "Donald Trump's Chances of Winning Are Approaching Zero." Adding to the dismal polls, outrage over the many questionable statements, and the *Access Hollywood* tape, was the growing narrative about Russia.

Following a release by Wikileaks of Democratic National Campaign emails that allegedly came from Russian hackers, whispers became louder that there was collusion between the Trump campaign and Russia. *Time* led with a summer headline, "Donald Trump's Many, Many, Many, Many Ties to Russia." In the heightened media spotlight, campaign manager Paul Manafort resigned partially due to stories alleging links to foreign entities in August 2016. He was subsequently investigated by Special Counsel Robert Mueller and jailed; Trump pardoned him during his first term.

One underestimated undercurrent was that Hillary Clinton was not well-accepted by voters who had supported her primary opponent, Bernie Sanders. Sanders was akin to a populist on the Democratic side and had mirrored Trump's positions on trade, worker rights, and the border for many years, though overall, his ideological approach to politics contrasted strongly with Trump's. On election day, November 8, 2016, the picture became clearer as the night went on. States not considered in play began to go to the Republican candidate. Pennsylvania. Michigan. Wisconsin. Donald Trump would become the 45th president of the United States. MAGA was on its way to Washington, DC.

President Trump

Donald J. Trump was inaugurated on January 20, 2017, with the political establishment still in shock. Overall, the first Trump term was characterized by chaos and constant struggle. Yet, there were notable domestic and foreign policy milestones in the mix. This period also fostered a group of allies who would form the backbone of the new Republican Party.

Initial Days

During those early days of the first Trump administration, the media consistently conveyed that Trump was not a legitimate president. Many arguments were made to buttress this contention. One was that he lost the popular vote. Another was that the voters were misled, either willfully by foreign powers or through political manipulation. According to most political pundits, Trump's extreme rhetoric should have dissuaded the electorate from choosing him.

The narrative of Trump as a Manchurian candidate at Russia's behest also had built-in appeal and gained steam. It moved from a conspiracy theory to the centerpiece of an FBI investigation—codenamed Crossfire Hurricane—that began at the end of the Obama administration and continued into Trump's term. The investigation climaxed with a report by Robert Mueller, a special counsel appointed by then-Deputy Attorney General Rod Rosenstein. Ultimately, the notion that Trump was a proxy Putin candidate was discarded politically, except in partisan circles, where the idea of illegitimacy persists to this day.

The level of scrutiny early on meant that any politician seeking to join the administration was under a cloud. There was a revolving door of appointments and an endless stream of leaks. Every development seemed to morph into a potentially apocalyptic scenario.

Everyone was asked to pick a side, whether the matter was the Brett Kavanaugh nomination, Ukraine, or the border wall. There was exhaustion in political circles and throughout the public more generally. When Chief of Staff John Kelly resigned at the end of 2018, it seemed to signal that the Trump administration was in serious turmoil.

Second Half

Nevertheless, heading into the 2020 election year, Trump was quite formidable. He held his highest approval ratings since entering office. Rates of unemployment were at record lows across demographics. The world was getting used to the new style of American politics. Trump even seemed to move past the attempt at impeachment, which was related to military aid to Ukraine.

While criticized in foreign policy circles, Trump's visit to North Korea and meeting with its ruler Kim Jung Un was undoubtedly bold. It demonstrated that Trump was starting to chart his own way forward—a foreign policy frame of peace through strength. In 2019, by enacting targeted sanctions, he blocked the Nord Stream 2 gas pipeline that Russia was building to Germany. In 2020, his son-in-law, Jared Kushner, helped orchestrate the Abraham Accords, which bolstered normalization between Israel and the Arab states of Morocco, Bahrain, and the United Arab Emirates.

Domestically, before the height of the pandemic, the White House was also making headway in its tariff standoff with China. That development dovetailed with increased manufacturing jobs. Meanwhile Congress approved extensive tax cuts, delivering on a key part of the White House's platform. It seemed that a Trump agenda was underway.

The second half of 2020, however, played out very differently. The COVID-19 pandemic and the subsequent response became a combined force that shook America's (and the world's) political, social, and economic underpinnings. It was not just the deaths from the disease. Tens of millions of people lost their livelihoods overnight. Schools shut down. The economy almost ground to a halt.

With an election cycle coming up, political battle lines became more pronounced. America's cities rose up in fiery protests after the death of George Floyd. The Black Lives Matter movement that emerged became a powerful mobilizing force. Heading into the election in November 2020, America's streets were on fire, its hospitals were full, and its workplaces empty. Trump was on the back foot.

Exit

The Republican Party generally coalesced around Trump as the 2020 candidate, but there was also a countermovement within the GOP that mobilized against him. While this may have limited some of Trump's reach, a more impactful factor was the expansion of mail-in ballots, which enabled greater Democratic mobilization and for which the Republican Party machine was unprepared.

Mail-in ballots and the conditions resulting from the COVID-19 pandemic delayed voting counts across contested states. While the election was held on November 3, the results were not declared across most media platforms until November 7. What transpired in the weeks after caused a fissure within the Republican Party.

Ultimately, while recounts were undertaken in select counties, the Electoral College confirmed the Biden victory in December 2020, making the January 6, 2021, certification a formality. Of course, it was anything but that in the end, as covered earlier. The events of that day led to the arrests of over 1,500 people. All eventually received clemency under the second Trump presidency.

What happened on January 6, 2021, and how it evolved became part of the same narrative from the entire first Trump term. What one side saw as a scandal or crisis was depicted by the other as a hoax. Whether it was Russia, Charlottesville, or January 6, each political group had two distinct sets of facts, valid or otherwise. Thus, the presidency ended as it began, with a dueling set of perspectives.

Opposition Trump

When Trump left the White House on January 20, 2021, he refused to attend the inauguration of his successor, Joe Biden. The Biden administration immediately began reversing Trump's executive orders and, in light of the events of January 6, joined with allies in the Republican Party to marginalize the MAGA movement and its backers.

With Trump in convalescence after the election and seemingly ostracized, the Republican Party appeared ready to move on. He had also lost his bully pulpit after being banished in a coordinated fashion from social media, where he held tremendous sway. Following his presidency, his brand was seemingly tarnished, and his name did not hold the same value.

Trump's business interests were also under pressure, and it appeared his political career might be over. He retreated to Mar-a-Lago. For most of 2021, he was rarely seen or heard from. Yet, his supporters did not leave him. For Trump himself, there was renewed clarity on who was truly part of the inner circle of the MAGA movement. While from afar, it appeared Trump had left the scene, in retrospect, he was regrouping. In his mind, there was unfinished business. TMTG, the holding company for Truth Social, was formed within a month of Trump's leaving office in early 2021.

While Trump was returning to social media on his own platform in early 2022, Elon Musk suddenly bid for Twitter in April that same year, acquiring it by October. Separately, in Mar-a-Lago, the former president was consolidating his close team of loyal personnel, a great deal of whom have since been appointed to the White House to serve in the administration during his second term.

Trump also took stock of the policies and principles that guided his first term. In light of the performance of the Biden administration, the former president was able to articulate a coherent perspective of his presidency's accomplishments in contrast—and what he would restore if he returned. He outlined part of this in a speech delivered to supporters of the conservative think tank, the Heritage Foundation, in April 2022, highlighting the issues of the border, wars, and the economy.

With the midterm elections upcoming in 2022, there was growing concern around Trump's opposition role in Democratic and establishment Republican circles. At the time, the star of Florida Republican Governor Ron DeSantis was rising nationally. DeSantis was seen by his team as a more effective executive than Trump. He formed a PAC to contest the Republican primary in May 2022. Trump, however, would not relent and began his journey in earnest as the de facto opposition leader in America. It became apparent that he would seek the Republican nomination, which he declared on November 15, 2022.

The United States v. Trump

Until that point, the Department of Justice had not earnestly undertaken legal investigations of the former president. That changed following Trump's announcement, and Jack Smith was appointed as Special Counsel by Attorney General Merrick Garland on November 18, 2022, to probe impropriety by Trump on a number of fronts. Soon, a flurry of civil and criminal, state and federal legal investigations were initiated against the former president, concluding in formal indictments and even convictions.

In the end, both federal indictments and stage charges were filed against the former president. At the federal level, Smith brought two cases to court. One involved the alleged mishandling of classified documents. The search warrant for that indictment led to a raid on the former president's residence at Mar-a-Lago, during which the personal effects of Melania Trump were searched. This has stayed in the president's mind and influenced his opinion of the FBI, which conducted the search. The case was dismissed in the summer of 2024, although it was under appeal before the Department of Justice dropped it in light of Trump's win.

The second case related to Trump's role in the events of January 6, 2021, but it faced legal hurdles. The Supreme Court ruled that the president's official acts are not covered by Department of Justice oversight. Ultimately, the case was moot and wound down after Trump's re-election.

In Georgia, a RICO, or racketeering, case was filed against Trump and a number of co-defendants for conspiring to overturn the 2020 election result. The prosecutor in that case was disqualified for impropriety. While this is currently under appeal, the overall proceedings are also indefinitely paused.

In New York, the state's case related to the falsification of business records concerning a payment to the adult actress Stormy Daniels. While he was convicted on 34 counts, legal analysts suggested that the ruling might be reversed upon appeal. Trump's appearance in the Manhattan courtroom only seemed to raise his profile, and his mugshot, which went viral, now hangs outside the Oval Office.

Separately, the New York State attorney general successfully sued the Trump Organization and its owners, the Trump family, for inflating the value of assets when obtaining loans. An appeal is still pending in this case, and the eventual resolution may take years.

These legal cases fell under the same spell as the more controversial political moments during Trump's first term. For his followers, they were just more examples of how the proverbial establishment was trying to prevent Trump's return to the presidency. Polling showed a majority of Republican voters believed the former president was being targeted for political reasons, regardless of the evidence being presented in the courts.

The Return

Ron DeSantis formally entered the Republican primary on May 24, 2023. He would later be joined by seven other candidates who met the criteria to join the first debate outside of Trump: former governors Nikki Haley, Doug Burgum, Chris Christie, and Asa Hutchinson; former Vice President Mike Pence; Senator Tim Scott; and wildcard entrepreneur Vivek Ramaswamy. There were five debates, with the final one coming just before the Iowa Caucuses in January 2024.

Trump did not participate in a single debate, yet he consistently led in the polls. After he won decisively in Iowa, all but one of the candidates—Nikki Haley—dropped out heading into the New Hampshire primary later that month. The New Hampshire primary allowed for non-GOP voters, so the final count was closer than anticipated. This gave life to the Never Trump movement and encouraged others outside the party to back Haley. Haley eventually suspended her campaign in March but did not formally endorse Trump until the Republican Convention in July.

In late April, Trump met privately with DeSantis to coordinate on strategy. A portion of the GOP donor base had bolstered DeSantis's candidacy, and Trump's direct attacks on the governor—often in his regular no-holds-barred style—caused a lot of ill will between the two camps. While DeSantis spoke at the convention, he was not a very visible surrogate in the campaign. It was clear that Trump was consolidating his own political apparatus, apart from even the new guard that had joined the DeSantis team. This precipitated, in part, a second evolution of the GOP since Trump came to the fore, further solidifying the MAGA movement in place of others in the party.

While Pence, Haley, and Christie have faded from view, Tim Scott is still an ally in the Senate, and Ramaswamy and Burgum joined Trump on the campaign trail. This led to an administration appointment for Burgum and a preliminary engagement of Ramaswamy in the newly created Department of Government Efficiency before he declared his intention to run for governor of Ohio.

Winning the Republican primary was just the start for Trump. Yet, just as in 2016, Trump began to overcome obstacles as they emerged. First up was the sitting president and presumptive Democratic nominee, Joe Biden. The debate between the two candidates was held earlier than normal, at the end of June.

Biden's debate performance was so worrying for the Democratic Party that it kicked off a sustained campaign to replace him as a candidate. This was difficult because the Democratic primaries had already concluded. The way those primaries were held, with no debates, also meant that there was no real second-place successor to stand in for the nomination.

Then, on July 13, at a political rally in Butler, Pennsylvania, a lone gunman took aim at Donald Trump while he was on stage. In a twist of fate, the former president turned his head in the nick of time and was only clipped on the ear. One bystander was killed, and two others were critically injured. It was the first such incident in decades. In the immediate aftermath, Trump stood up defiantly and yelled to the crowd, "Fight, fight, fight!"

Immediately after that assassination attempt, there was a change in the mood of latent supporters who had stood on the sidelines. That same day, Elon Musk endorsed Donald Trump for president. Mark Zuckerberg praised Trump's response to the attempt, calling him a "badass." This also led to a conversation between Robert F. Kennedy Jr., or RFK Jr., who was by then an independent candidate in the presidential race, and Trump.

Emboldened by these events, Trump selected then-Senator JD Vance as his running mate over other names, doubling down on the MAGA movement within the Republican Party. With that momentum shift, Trump seemed triumphant at the Republican National Convention in Milwaukee the following week. However, the coronation was short-lived. Joe Biden dropped out of the race several days later due to pressure within the Democratic Party and endorsed Vice President Kamala Harris as the nominee. The race had shifted from an older Biden to a younger Harris as Trump's opponent.

In the end, it did not matter. There was a consolidation of rivals and movements under the MAGA movement and Trump's leadership. RFK Jr.—who had sought the Democratic nomination and was the only independent candidate in the race of note—endorsed Trump for president. He would bring former Democratic voters with him as well as disenchanted independents.

Trump's Madison Square Garden rally was held one week before the election. It featured a diverse lineup that included figures who would later join his administration. In addition to regular MAGA stalwarts, there were new political allies and old friends: RFK Jr., media star Tucker Carlson, former Democratic presidential candidate Tulsi Gabbard, wrestler Hulk Hogan, UFC founder Dana White, and Elon Musk.

During the rally, a comedian made crude remarks about Puerto Rico, which caused a media firestorm. But this time, the effect was limited. One reason for this was that the Trump campaign had heavily tapped into alternative media, and its message was dominating among its potential voters, especially young Gen Z men.

In the campaign's final months, with guidance from his youngest son, Barron, and campaign advisor Alex Bruesewitz, Trump appeared on leading podcasts and, eventually, *The Joe Rogan Experience*. The reach was immense and ultimately crowded out noise from other media. This meant that going into the election, Trump had garnered the backing of new groups of voters and donors who were not present in 2020 and 2016. This was not Trump 1.0 or even 2.0. It was something more.

Trump 2.5

Donald Trump decisively defeated Kamala Harris and was declared the winner by media outlets on election night. There had been a feeling it would take several days to determine a winner. However, this was not the case. Trump also became the first Republican candidate to win the popular vote in two decades.

Given the dynamics at play, Trump's electoral win in 2024 was not a surprise. Yet it was still a shock. Scenes of chaos on January 6, 2021, criminal indictments, civil judgments, denigration in the press, and the risk of death—throughout it all, Trump remained standing. If the question of his legitimacy and his mandate from an informed electorate had been open, it was now definitely closed.

Trump entered the White House in 2025 as only the second president, after Grover Cleveland, to serve a non-consecutive second term. Following everything that has happened, he feels emboldened. The second term is not a redux of the first term and the return of President Trump. It is entirely different.

Trump 2.5 is not just a catchy moniker. It reflects an additional level of awareness, ability, and urgency built into the second Trump administration. Since Trump declared his candidacy in November 2022, momentum had been building around developing the policy proposals and personnel for a potential victory. Once that election victory came in November 2024, the idea was to hit the ground running from November 6 and not wait until inauguration day.

If President Trump had won re-election in 2020, it would have been a continuation of the first term, with slightly more accomplishments, the same fecklessness, and infighting to jockey for the future of the Republican Party. It would have been Trump 2.0. Regardless, Trump's return to the White House was seemingly out of the cards.

Instead, in an almost Lazarus-like moment, Trump's return and decisive victory gives him an unprecedented mandate. His organization has clear capabilities that were missing in the first term. The current president is no ordinary second-term president. He has had four years to regroup, understand who his opponents are, and ensure that there is an effective team. The trials and tribulations he faced also led to newfound allies beyond the inner group from 2016 and 2020.

Underestimating the depth of decision-making that will take place and the capabilities to execute those decisions comes at the peril of Trump's opponents. Trump 2.5 means taking Trump at his word, taking his administration seriously, and appreciating his team's rigor. It also means accepting a neglected aspect: This White House entered with a popular mandate.

The results of the election on November 5, 2024 mean that voters elected Trump to enact the very policies he is implementing. The political platform he campaigned on was transparent about what policies would be carried out, even on controversial positions around dismantling the bureaucracy and pardoning January 6 prisoners. While opponents may claim this is wrong, the voters elected this mandate and Trump, knowing all that he is.

III

PRINCIPLES AND POLICIES

Following Donald J. Trump's inauguration as the 47th President of the United States on January 20, 2025, there was no time lost in enacting his agenda. At his Victory Rally at the Capitol Arena in Washington, DC, he began signing executive orders with immediate effect, much to the pleasure of the crowd. The signal was clear: The Trump 2.5 era means business.

Yet, there is still a lack of clarity about what that signifies exactly. President Trump's innumerable statements make a coherent reading of policy difficult. In addition, as he is always in a state of negotiation, it is at times unclear what his fundamental positions are versus what is intended to shift the goalposts for a future deal.

The second Trump administration also has new policies and perspectives. Some issues, such as artificial intelligence, did not have prominence during the first term. Nevertheless, the White House is generally guided by the same philosophy, principles, and imperatives that have been part of the MAGA platform since its inception. Additionally, while no single document outlines the Trump 2.5 era in-depth, this chapter is informed by a clear reading of events, statements, and actions.

Philosophy

The overarching philosophy of the Trump 2.5 era is America First. While seemingly a slogan, it encapsulates the essence that guides the administration's decision-making. It goes beyond the aspiration of 'Make America Great Again' to become a matrix or filter through which every decision or issue can pass. Even if there are new crises, it is still the filter.

This is helpful because the next four years will be uncharted territory. In addition, there will be debates and contesting interpretations even within the Trump administration. When that occurs, observers and staffers alike will benefit from returning to the preeminent philosophy of America First to understand where things may end up.

If an international organization has American funding, the Trump administration will continue it only if the institution does not relegate American interests to a second position. Similarly, in a bilateral relationship, any trade deficit is seen as negative. If two parties ask America to intervene in a conflict, evaluating which side benefits the United States will be essential. If an ally seeks intervention, they will need to ensure it is in the American interest.

Is this necessarily new? Arguably, it has been the basis for American policy for decades. In 1991, the United States intervened in the Gulf War on Kuwait's side. While ideological motivations existed, Kuwait compensated the United States with billions of dollars.

The current disposition is a more explicit—and perhaps aggressive—articulation of a long-standing American strategy to ensure dominance. If a country, trade relationship, or geopolitical flashpoint benefits a rival of America, the U.S. under Trump will set out to reverse that, regardless of norms or international precedents. Thus, if the Panama Canal benefits China more than the United States, this will always be a red flag.

Over an extended time horizon, this philosophy faces more complexity in application. A policy that is America First in the short term could cause long-term detriment. Another challenge is that applying an America First philosophy in one arena might undermine cooperation in another.

Perhaps the greatest challenge comes from special interests. In the 1980s and 1990s, the United States ushered China into the World Trade Organization, promoting a clear pathway for American companies to outsource manufacturing to China, where they benefited from cheap labor. Ultimately, this led to a sharp fall in domestic manufacturing, decimating local communities and creating national security risks in key sectors.

Special interests—in this case, American corporations—promoted a bipartisan agenda that lasted for decades. The same could be said across a number of industries today, from agriculture to pharmaceuticals to weapons. As the Trump administration ventures into policy debates, relying on corporate executives and specialized constituencies in the MAGA coalition for input, it will need to carefully weigh what is America First and what is 'special interests' first.

Critics of the 47th president assert that America First is a cloak for these special interests. Ultimately, this litmus test will be put to voters in the midterm elections of 2026.

Principles

The principles underlying the Trump administration, the MAGA movement, and the America First philosophy are not easy to delineate. This primer distills them into a set of five: strength, sovereignty, efficiency, modernization, and traditionalism.

Strength

The overriding principle is for the United States to be a strong country, domestically and globally. As an already dominant country, this translates to two things. First, it means being the strongest country in practical terms and maintaining that position vis-à-vis others. Second, it means maximizing its strength to its utmost potential.

The second point is essential to note. Across a range of industries, the United States is already in the pole position, for example as the largest oil producer. However, this is not good enough. If it is not doing as well as it should, the Trump administration will identify strategies to improve. It is not enough to be the strongest; the objective is to continually deepen strength in all arenas.

Strength is cultivated across sectors, whether geopolitical, political, economic, technological, or cultural. There is nuance, and it is about more than just brute force. In the eyes of the Trump administration, strength is capability and effectiveness.

Geopolitically, America needs to be able to outmaneuver and outflank its lesser rivals, China and Russia. This includes investing in weapons capabilities that ensure American dominance. It also suggests participating in alliances that give America the dexterity to project force where it needs to. Reducing commitments in one theater and deploying them elsewhere may be necessary.

What strength implies at a domestic political level is more challenging to articulate because of America's bipartisan nature and the separation of powers and levels of government. Yet, strength in this arena translates to the executive's power to get things done in an unobstructed fashion. When a decision is made, it should be enacted throughout the system.

Economically, this principle can be fraught when translated into policy positions. Take the American dollar as an example. A weak dollar enables more exports due to cheaper goods, helping the U.S. reverse its trade deficits with other countries. A stronger dollar makes the U.S. a destination for investment and increases the value of assets. It also provides the U.S. with tremendous buying power around the world.

Economic strength is most accurately depicted in two ways: return on labor and return on capital. Can investors generate returns, and can American workers generate sufficient livelihoods? This has to be true across socioeconomic classes and over long periods.

Technologically, strength is about competitive advantage and being on the frontier of innovation. Again, this is a challenge in today's hyper-financialized age. Is an American company necessarily at the forefront of innovation because it has a high valuation? Does its market positioning due in part to excess capital mean that this is a net good for the advancement of technology? These debates might be most acute in the AI sector.

Strength in culture may be the hardest to define. Yet the strength of the nation, not just the state, is a fundamental principle of the Trump administration and the MAGA movement. There is a push for unity and highlighting the shared traits between citizens, which is in contrast with the mantra of strength through diversity. The question is, does unity mean uniformity? American cultural vibrancy and production have been some of its biggest assets over the past century. Investing in that would be a net good, but it comes with the subjectivity of defining a cultural asset.

Across the board, the notion of a strong America and investing in strength is a recurring theme regardless of the issue or policy in question.

Sovereignty

The second principle, interrelated with the first, is sovereignty. It is vital to elevate, safeguard, and advance American sovereignty. This does not stop with the homeland but extends to everything American, including citizens and assets abroad, anywhere and everywhere.

Sovereignty starts with having a real and respected border. Sovereignty is undermined when the border is not robust, and the government cannot effectively control entry into the country. The counter to this is that the border is simply uncontrollable and that the U.S., by law, has obligations that necessitate an open border. Whether that interpretation is accurate or not, a preponderance of the electorate has rejected it.

Thus, for the Trump administration, absolute dominion over the territory of the United States is a first-order principle and is seen as eminently achievable. There are no exceptions to this. In practice, all entry and exit of individuals must be legal. If it is not, it will be contested.

There is a secondary implication: Sovereignty will be leveraged to enable the best possible return for America. Access to the American market and assets will not be 'free.' There will be a cost to accessing American sovereignty, including for immigrants.

The international inviolability of American persons—citizens and corporations—flows from the same principle of sovereignty. This principle also applies to American assets, whether physical in nature, including military bases or ships, or more intangible systems, such as the status of the U.S. dollar. The notion of sovereignty abroad conveys that attacks on citizens, corporations, or assets are equivalent to attacks on the homeland. Thus, Americans being held as prisoners by foreign governments is seen as a red line.

Past administrations treated the defense of American allies as sacrosanct. However, this does not necessarily apply within the sovereignty principle. A Trump administration will evaluate defending its sovereignty differently from defending anything outside its sovereignty. Of course, the principle of strength may still necessitate a clear response.

Efficiency

An America that cannot perform or get things done will be seen not as America First but rather America Last. Following the prerequisites of strength and sovereignty, how America functions or builds becomes paramount. The key to this is efficiency.

An efficient America runs properly and quickly in all facets of its government—from systems to services. This has three dimensions: one, the ability to carry out a function, task, or project from start to conclusion to the fullest extent (and well); two, the speed at which this is done; and three, the cost of doing it.

Each government agency or body is being evaluated and assessed across these dimensions. Service-level assessments are already taking place, big and small, to measure ability, speed, and cost. In some instances, the existing nature of a government body or set of regulations makes it impossible to carry out a task quickly and at a low cost. In those cases, the answer may not be reform but simply the cancellation of regulations or bodies. Institutions could disappear overnight or become defunct. This is much more difficult in practice, with most institutions empowered or funded by Congress.

The efficiency principle at the federal level will naturally translate to the devolution of processes and responsibilities to the state and local levels, making the federal government less of an encumbrance. However, a middle ground will be needed—not everything is able to proceed without federal oversight.

For instance, while the Trump administration may eliminate environmental regulations to facilitate quicker energy permits, negative externalities could arise. The argument would be that the current architecture is broken and debilitating. Thus, the efficiency principle has inherent contradictions over an extended period that will only be resolved by subjective decision-making and value preferences.

Finally, efficiency—getting things done—will require the full exercise of the government's power. This will become increasingly relevant regarding infrastructure and matters of eminent domain, which may raise libertarian criticism about individual rights. This has yet to be fully negotiated within Republican circles.

Modernization

America is at the forefront in many sectors, but in others, it has lagged behind leading global economies. Modernization refers to updating and upgrading the American economy and infrastructure to make it the most competitive globally.

This principle is the hardest to implement because it relies on the private sector advancing public interest and the public sector performing in ways it has not in decades. While the presidency has significant power, Congress is responsible for the size and scope of any budget allocation. In addition, modernization is not just the federal government's purview. It would involve the states and municipalities.

Modernization seeks to put America in the pole position in the technological age in frontier sectors like space, artificial intelligence, decentralized finance, and medicine. That will mean that the education sector, government-sponsored research centers, and affiliated initiatives will become laser-focused on this goal. In the administration's eyes, obstacles to modernization, such as DEI, must be relegated to the side.

Modernization also pertains to government performance and the ability to deliver services, which act as a bulwark to the principle of efficiency. Thus, technology enables government modernization, which, in effect, enables government efficiency. However, this could lead to decreased services and a reduced government workforce.

In addition to emphasizing technology and government performance, the modernization of America's infrastructure is a priority. Ultimately, the modernization of the electricity grid, power capabilities, roads and bridges, and transportation networks will lay the groundwork for American strength and sovereignty today and in the future.

Notable challenges exist, including the cost required for such projects. Examples of grand infrastructure projects in the past include NASA's space program in the 1950s and 1960s and the Eisenhower-led highway system. More recently, the Inflation Reduction Act along with the Bipartisan Infrastructure Law constitute the largest pieces of infrastructure legislation in recent memory. They also included renewable energy projects under the umbrella of the Green New Deal, which Trump has labeled the "green new scam."

Modernization, however, is more straightforward as an idea. Taking a project to completion, especially larger infrastructure projects, is all about the details, which are only discovered in implementation.

Traditionalism

While most principles have a tangible component, where the government has a clear role, the final one is more abstract. Traditionalism relates to restoring a past ideal of what American culture and the family represent. It has been part and parcel of the MAGA movement.

At the heart is the stated advancement of the family unit and the protection of children. There is pushback against any dilution of gender, and the complete restoration of the binary construct of male and female is central. Any public or government recognition or sponsorship of any other gender construct is null and void.

Promoting the family unit and the role of the family in America is a basic tenet within the principle of traditionalism. The sponsorship of abortion is being restricted, and in its place, policies that promote marriage and children are being forwarded. This includes affirmative programs, namely funding for in vitro fertilization (IVF).

There is a purported big tent perspective underlying the America First philosophy and MAGA movement that would at least partially contradict past conservative positions. Several top officials appointed by Trump are gay. In addition, on the campaign trail it was clear that there would be no federal abortion ban. Thus, the principle is best distilled to mean that the traditional family unit will be promoted officially, but trade-offs will have to be made when implementing policy, given the complexities in practice and political considerations.

Many of the specifics around traditionalism depend on the president and his direction. While the government may avoid more hardline positions, public sentiment driven by the MAGA movement may still lead to a negative or hostile environment for marginalized groups.

Foreign Policy

There is no clear path for American foreign policy in the Trump 2.5 era. The best way to think about America's international relations over the next four years is to imagine a complex multi-stakeholder decision tree. Depending on the choices made by countries regarding President Trump's new approach, this could lead to deals or confrontations.

This will play out concurrently across all regions. The confluence of this never-ending flow of developments will continually reorient interests and alliances. It will then precipitate second-order events that seem to come out of nowhere, presenting new challenges and opportunities.

Although this may create a feeling of randomness, Trump's foreign policy is based on the America First philosophy, associated principles, and imperatives. While there are common themes, the approach favors policy at a bilateral level. Over four decades, a few global issues have reverberated in Trump's platforms, political discourse, and interviews that merit attention.

Imperatives

Foreign policy is driven by the underlying America First philosophy and the principles of strength, sovereignty, efficiency, modernization, and traditionalism. Additional imperatives are at the forefront: advancing American prosperity, peace through strength, and balance of power.

Advancing American Prosperity

American prosperity is a foremost aim at all times. This imperative is emphasized in each bilateral relationship and the entire foreign policy approach will be evaluated through this lens. How do all relationships, memberships, alliances, and other forms of cooperation advance American prosperity?

Today, America's annual trade deficit reaches nearly $1 trillion. Many economists have contended that this is not bad for the world and that, ultimately, the U.S. is able to import inexpensive goods, thereby helping its consumers. The Trump administration sees this as a negative for manifold reasons. Firstly, from a pure numbers standpoint, America is buying more than it is selling and, thus, is trading at a loss. Secondly, while consumers may save money on specific goods, the decimation of American manufacturing capabilities undermines American prosperity and security. Finally, workers in America in the manufacturing class have been hit hardest.

The jury will be out to see whether other countries are receptive to eliminating trade deficits. This negotiation will primarily be driven by tariff stand-offs. These could severely disrupt supply chains and increase prices for many goods. They could encourage the formation of economic alliances against the United States as a response.

Advancing American prosperity also constitutes securing access, global infrastructure, and supply routes that benefit America rather than its rivals. The cases of Greenland and the Panama Canal, with their proximity to the United States and its close sphere of influence, become critical. This does not mean asserting direct rule by the United States but rather enforcing agreements that ensure all its economic needs are met and that its rivals—notably China—are sidelined.

Finally, the sovereignty principle is an interrelated aspect of the American prosperity imperative. Under the Trump administration, the American private sector operating internationally is seen as an extension of America. It, therefore, operates under the protection of American sovereignty. Thus, moves against American companies, even under the auspices of foreign legal proceedings, will induce a direct response. This occurred during the first Trump administration when France imposed a digital services tax that would have reduced the profits of American companies; this was met with the immediate threat of retaliatory American tariffs.

Peace Through Strength

The peace-through-strength formula has been articulated multiple times by Trump, his Secretary of State Marco Rubio, Secretary of Defense Pete Hegseth, and numerous others. It was ultimately what many in the MAGA movement attributed to the absence of a Russian attack on Ukraine during Trump's first term.

The notion is that peace is maintained through America's ability to act decisively and forcefully against its enemies to defend its interests. As Chairman of the Joint Chiefs of Staff, Colin Powell implemented the overwhelming force doctrine, sometimes known as the Powell doctrine. This doctrine was exercised during the Gulf War from 1990 to 1991.

While the Powell Doctrine is about establishing prerequisites that ensure absolute asymmetry before military action is authorized, it is similar to the peace-through-strength formula. It is no accident that the Gulf War was seen as a demonstration of American power in the post-Cold War order. In effect, it gave way to American supremacy in the Middle East. That, of course, only led to new insurgent enemies, principally Al Qaeda, raising questions on how to define strength in an asymmetric world.

The peace-through-strength doctrine builds on the Powell doctrine. It seeks to ensure American military supremacy at all times, in all theatres, and for any eventuality. In addition, it is exercised—as in the case of the assassination of Iranian general Qassem Suleimani in 2020—on an ongoing basis. Thus, it must be understood that Trump is not an anti-war president necessarily. If there is a threat against America and an enemy does not back down, Trump will exercise military force. However, the theory is that the threat of force, over time, will be enough to compel American adversaries to sue for peace and make deals.

Balance of Power

The Trump administration is not receding into isolationism by peeling back from American universality. Instead, it seeks to re-establish a new balance of power that reflects the nature of the world as the administration sees it. China has risen as a second power. In addition, there are new middling powers that, while under the American umbrella, are close to usurping or matching the level of many European countries, namely India, Indonesia, Turkey, and perhaps Saudi Arabia. And then there is the long-standing rival, Russia.

The post-World War II order that led to the bipolar bifurcation of the international scene gave way to an American global order after 1991. The Trump administration still sees America as the dominant power and believes that American dominance should be maintained. However, it also sees the limitations of America as a pseudo-imperial entity.

As such, the Trump administration is following the imperative to create a more sustainable balance of power, as it sees it. That entails negotiating with China and demarcating interests. It is the same with Russia. Thus, there would be an equation established to make clear where American interests are paramount and where Chinese and Russian interests are deferred to, particularly closer to their borders.

Global Issues

The Trump 2.5 foreign policy approach gives precedence to bilateral relationships foremost and downplays the multilateral system and even regional alliances. The perspective is that those modalities mask the underlying nature of power. Thus, the Trump administration would underscore only a few global issues that have multilateral dimensions. Three are worth highlighting: nuclear non-proliferation, conflict mitigation, and global de-governance. Trump has echoed all multiple times—before running, during his first term, and since. They are also anchored in numerous policy documents.

Nuclear Non-proliferation

There is arguably no issue that Trump has raised more often than nuclear non-proliferation when it comes to foreign policy. In his many interviews, dating back to the 1980s, and even in his book outlining his formal political platform in 2000, he labeled this as the greatest threat to the world. Following his first administration, Trump revealed that he had been in the beginning stages of discussions with Russia to de-nuclearize to the fullest extent possible and that he believed China would join any subsequent discussions.

This may sound far-fetched. However, it is the one global issue that Trump will probably be engaged in. The contradiction will, of course, be that the U.S. will still seek

Principles and Policies

to have the most advanced nuclear capabilities to ensure its dominance through the peace-through-strength formula. Regardless, the energy around global treaties for the Sustainable Development Goals (SDGs) and climate change will be partially re-channeled by this administration to nuclear non-proliferation.

Conflict Mitigation

Conflict mitigation will, at times, play out haphazardly but, in general, is being pursued by the administration globally. There are two exceptions. Where America is confronting its rivals and emerging threats, it will act decisively, forcefully, and, if required, militarily. It will likely back select allies in such contexts, notably Israel. When conflict breaks out in regions that are not of concern to the United States, the Trump administration will not want to risk blood and treasure to restore calm. Instead, it will devolve responsibility to regional powers.

Nevertheless, the Trump administration will proactively resolve conflicts in flashpoints and regions of importance. This is true in the Middle East, the Korean Peninsula, and Eastern Europe and applies to South Asia. If there were a skirmish between Pakistan and India, there would be quick intervention. That being said, some scenarios could lead to escalation. This is most likely in Gaza, which remains unresolved, marked only by temporary cessations of violence. Given the strong relationship that the administration has with Israel, it will be more permissive of military activity if Hamas does not leave the territory.

The military will reduce its footprint in regions not considered fundamental to prevent potential conflict involving U.S. forces. This is already happening in Africa.

Global De-governance

The Trump administration champions global de-governance to encourage devolved responsibility and a new balance of power. If the Obama and Biden administrations were characterized by building and investing in the institutional fabric of an international rules-based order, the Trump 2.5 policy is about dismantling it and fostering a new architecture.

What does this mean in practice? Except for the most inherent and intrinsic of treaties related to war and peace—such as nuclear weapons and chemical weapons—the Trump administration will evaluate all and decide whether to withdraw from or defund specific organizations. This might include the United Nations itself and other international agencies.

The global de-governance effort will be proactive. The idea is not that there is no prevailing order but instead countries and regions should 'police' their neighborhoods. Subsequently, a more synchronized set of rules will be encouraged relating to underlying power dynamics rather than U.S. involvement. In practice, this could lead to short-term chaos. Despite the rhetoric, select international institutions and legal treaties will remain backed by U.S. involvement, given their complex intractability.

Regions

Most of the Trump administration's foreign policy is carried out bilaterally. There is no preferential basis for allies; policy is enacted on a transactional basis. That said, multiple-issue alignments—including ideologically—will bring further co-operation and the semblance of an alliance. There is a more targeted strategy for rivals and adversaries.

Adversaries

In the Trump 2.5 era, there is zero tolerance for adverse actions by countries against American interests. Conversely, the administration stands ready to make so-called deals. This was clear during Trump's first term on the Korean Peninsula. Thus, the policy towards adversaries is containment as a primary action, confrontation, if necessary, retaliation when required, and détente preferred. One matter that cuts across individual adversaries is the challenge to the primacy of the American dollar, which is mainly led by China and Russia. The most salient example is the currency proposed by the BRICS bloc. This is a red line for the Trump administration, and it will use economic tools at its disposal to counteract a formal centralized currency as an alternative to the U.S. dollar.

CHINA

President Trump invited Chinese President Xi Jinping to his inauguration. While the Trump 2.5 stance aims to pull back from the universality of America's presence, it still seeks a monopoly of its interests in the Western Hemisphere. In addition, the Trump administration will endeavor to minimize and contain Chinese influence in geostrategic regions like the Gulf, African countries with critical supply chains, and Greenland, where there are critical supply chains for tomorrow.

If that containment is met, confrontation can be avoided. This is also the matter concerning China's provocations toward long-standing American allies Japan, Korea, and Taiwan. Ultimately, the Trump administration will view any American response through the lens of American prosperity. Trump will look to offer protection if relations with Taiwan, Japan, and Korea advance American prosperity but could otherwise defer to Chinese interests.

The containment of China does not extend to its regional influence. The Trump administration is less likely to be worried by Chinese influence throughout East Asia. Retaliation will likely only take place on trade and other matters, such as synthetic drugs, that directly threaten American sovereignty. Ultimately, Trump's goal appears to be a negotiated alignment with China.

Russia

Since his inauguration, President Trump has maintained a steady communication flow with President Putin and continues to pursue an all-encompassing restructuring of relations. A similar policy is being taken with Russia as with China, albeit with less consideration for any upside. China's economy is larger, giving it more sway. In addition, a stable relationship with China does much more to advance American prosperity.

Thus, the Trump administration's strategy might become forceful at points to ensure that Russia's ambitions are contained. Initially, the White House has taken a conciliatory outlook. While the main concern is Ukraine, the posture also pertains to Russian expansion of influence in the Middle East when seen as counter to U.S. interests. That will be the test of a Putin-led Russia in its relations with Trump's America. How does Putin respond to a deal that gives more regional latitude around its borders but also entails global deference to the United States?

Within Europe, Trump will develop security protections at the regional level. Even in Ukraine, the administration is not looking to back a complete restoration of Ukrainian sovereignty over Crimea or part of the eastern provinces. How this unfolds in bordering states comprising Georgia, Moldova, and elsewhere will be instructive.

There are not many issues where economic retaliation might arise vis-à-vis Russia. Perhaps this will occur in the energy file or other industries that significantly affect the American economy. Yet, overall, the trade relationship with Russia is limited. Thus, if there is a broad alignment, the Trump administration will favor rapid de-escalation overall and move towards resuming the discussion of denuclearization.

Iran

Simply put, Iran does not have the same stature as Russia and China. While President Trump may seek to be the first American president to visit Tehran in half a century, this will be seemingly impossible if the current leadership is in place. That being said, the death of Supreme Leader Ayatollah Khamenei, if it occurs while Trump is in office, would open new possibilities.

It is hard to see a grand bargain being struck, even if Iran's government sent positive signals about a reset with the Trump administration. Under the Trump administration, Israel is an ironclad ally. Iranian proxies are seen as implacable enemies. Many of Iran's senior officials are considered by the Trump administration as complicit in American deaths not just in the 1980s in Lebanon, during that country's civil war, but also in Iraq in the 2000s.

Thus, the current administration's immediate moves will likely mirror those of the first Trump term. They will target not just the containment of Iran and its proxies but potentially the castration of its capabilities in the region. The administration's position will be unyielding in response to any attacks against America, its allies, or its respective interests.

The door will remain open towards a conciliation, but the price would be extremely high. Such a rapprochement would presumably involve the dismantling of nuclear facilities, the dismemberment of all Iranian proxies, tens of billions of dollars for the compensation of past American deaths, and a pledge to integrate into America's security architecture.

Unlike with China and Russia, the Trump administration would require Iranian capitulation before a rapprochement. Thus, if there is to be a confrontation, it is most likely to occur with Iran.

Other States

There are other states outside the American orbit that are seen as smaller adversaries. Still, in contrast with the Biden administration, the Trump administration is grounded in an American First philosophy—not in an integrated rules-based order. Thus, states that are not democratic and do not participate in international institutions are of no concern to the Trump administration as long as American hegemony is respected in the Western hemisphere and other strategic interests are not threatened.

These adversarial states include North Korea, Venezuela, Belarus, Myanmar, Syria, Cuba, Yemen (under the Houthis), and Afghanistan (under the Taliban). In the beginning weeks of the Trump administration, many of these states sent positive overtures to the White House.

Altogether, relations with these countries will probably remain neither fully restored nor fully broken. In most cases, an unwritten equilibrium will be reached. There is a clear exception. As the U.S. in the Trump 2.5 era seeks Western hegemonic dominance, it will not accept Chinese influence in Cuba and Venezuela. In Cuba's case, given its proximity to the U.S. border, there may even be hints at regime change through economic pressure.

Regarding North Korea and Trump's emphasis on denuclearization—and what he sees as unfinished business from the first term—there will be an aggressive push to restore relations. It is unclear if the same supporting conditions exist in South Korea and the wider region as in the 2010s.

Non-State Actors

Regarding non-state actors, any actions taken against American citizens, military assets, or interests will be met with overwhelming force. Most non-state actors in this adversarial grouping are either Iranian proxies, anti-American Islamist terrorists, or both. This includes groups like Hezbollah, Hamas, Al Qaeda, the Houthis, Shabab, and ISIS.

Over the next four years, an onslaught of military activity to eliminate or weaken these groups is possible.

With respect to Hezbollah and Hamas, the U.S. will at times back Israel in its military confrontations with both. That being said, non-military means are preferred to achieve containment or disarmament of these groups. The year 2025 will be the test for this. If, for instance, Hezbollah begins to fire rockets against Israel, the Trump administration may see it as equivalent to an attack on American interests and respond accordingly.

Americas

The Trump administration is pursuing hegemonic dominance in the Western hemisphere. Countries with governments that have acted hostile to America—Venezuela and Cuba—will face the brunt of American pressure. How this plays out in the rest of Latin America might be a point of controversy. As with all bilateral relations, the same philosophy, principles, and imperatives constitute the filter.

Take the principle of American sovereignty. Countries that undermine American sovereignty, particularly in related to its southern border, will face pressure. Thus, the Central American countries of Guatemala, Honduras, El Salvador, and Nicaragua may have a 'one issue' relationship vis-à-vis the United States: immigration.

When it comes to Mexico and Canada, effectively direct border states, Trump will seek increased control in the relationships and a zero-tolerance policy for border violations. In addition, the goal of a balanced trade relationship remains without exceptions.

Europe+

The relationship with Europe is being evaluated both economically and ideologically. As the Trump administration seeks to forward its agenda, it will look for common cause with governments that share its agenda, notably Italy and Hungary. This could lead to new political movements taking power in some European countries to pursue closer relations with the United States under President Trump.

Given the multifaceted nature of each bilateral relationship with most countries, across a range of industries, it will feel like business as usual at times. However, each country, including Germany, France, and the United Kingdom, will undergo the same 'audit' of its trade relationship. In addition, when European countries seek to counteract Trump's global moves, whether regarding American adversaries or on issues such as social restoration, climate change, or migration, the White House may signal action against those countries. If they were to be seen as interfering domestically and politically in America, that would lead to a more blistering response.

Concerning the European Commission and European Union, the Trump administration will seek to defend American sovereignty when it comes to American companies. If the EU or EC fines a company, the Trump administration will retaliate, just as happened in the first term. If they seek to regulate American technology in a way that contradicts U.S. policy, there will be a robust response.

Finally, specific files are at the fore. Foremost is the Ukraine War and a repositioning of relations with Russia. Second is Greenland, which the Trump administration has identified as a national security concern. In both cases, the administration seeks economic and mineral rights. If Europe closes itself to American companies, energy, or products, America will remove its security guarantees. Thus, the idea of transactionality will supersede perceived alliances.

Middle East+

Like the Biden and Obama administrations, the Trump White House sees the Middle East as a secondary concern in a changing global landscape. Nevertheless, Israel's prime minister and Jordan's king were the first heads of state or government to visit the White House after the inauguration. The Middle East will still be at the forefront, even if other regions, namely the Americas, take precedence.

The objectives in the Middle East are threefold: removing security challenges for the U.S., ensuring American access to energy over rivals, and soliciting domestic investment. The U.S. sees security challenges to Israel as tantamount to challenges to the U.S. itself, and that will not change under Trump. However, that does not mean the president will indulge in all proactive actions that Israel takes, notably against Iran.

As noted, in an ideal scenario Trump intends to reach a sequel to the Joint Comprehensive Plan of Action (the Obama-era nuclear deal with Iran) that would end with the dismantlement of Iranian proxies and the defenestration of Iran's nuclear program. The administration will maintain an aggressive posture toward non-state militant groups but may acquiesce to engagement with Syria's political authorities. It will tolerate the presence of autocratic governments that support America's agenda.

Regarding the Israeli-Palestinian conflict, Trump continues to believe in expanding the Abraham Accords. While a lasting solution to the conflict would add a legacy element, overall calm and normalization of Israel are in the foreground at the outset. Unless there is a dramatic change in the Palestinian political fabric, that is all that is possible. That will not necessarily stop the president from offering bold—if not outlandish—proposals, among them American ownership of Gaza, as he did in February, to the shock of regional leaders.

In line with the Trump administration's policy favoring regionalized governance, the administration could probably foster a creative relationship with rising power Turkey regarding regional management. However, this will require careful consideration of Israel's and the Gulf's concerns.

Finally, investment is a concurrent target. In creating a sovereign wealth fund, the Trump administration will seek to partner with the largest sovereign wealth funds in the Gulf to bring investment into America. There will be a steady stream of private sector engagement, just as in the first term.

East and Southeast Asia

East and Southeast Asia are economically attractive to the United States, although China represents half of the combined region's GDP. The nature of the relationship can be seen through a trade and investment lens. While there will be security and defense arrangements with regional countries, they will not override the pursuit of a détente with China. Similarly, if denuclearization can be achieved in North Korea, it will take precedence over any regional objections.

Positive movement around China and the Korean Peninsula will create a pathway to a more transactional set of deals to advance American prosperity. Unlike in the Americas, where the top priority of the border creates tension, and in Europe, where there are ideological disagreements with the heart of the America First philosophy, Asian countries are much more ready to do business.

The relationship with Japan will have pre-eminence due to the size of the Japanese economy and President Trump's familiarity with the country. Its prime minister, one of the initial foreign leaders to visit the White House in 2025, is a successor to a friend of the president, Shinzo Abe, the former prime minister assassinated in 2022.

It will be interesting to observe how the U.S. evolves its economic ties with Southeast Asian countries that provide alternatives to European markets, namely Thailand, Indonesia, Malaysia, Vietnam, the Philippines, and Singapore, all of which have a nominal GDP near or exceeding $500 billion. In the first Trump term, officials criticized the Obama administration's so-called 'pivot to Asia' and the associated Trans-Pacific Partnership but did not provide an alternative framing.

South and Central Asia

Indian Prime Minister Narendra Modi was among the foreign leaders who visited Washington, DC, during Trump's first month in office, and his foreign minister attended the inauguration. In South Asia, India is the centerpiece of American engagement. It provides a pillar to counter Chinese and Russian influence.

This thinking is consistent with that of other administrations. In the Trump 2.5 era, however, things will presumably go further. In effect, deference to India's role within South Asia may take more precedence in the security architecture, given the U.S. retrenchment from that role. This would be more complex with regard to Pakistan, given the American military relationship and nuclear file there. But when it comes to smaller countries like Nepal, it is highly likely the Trump administration will defer to the Indian position on any matter that does not have national security implications for the U.S.

In Pakistan, the case of jailed political leader Imran Khan is a cause célèbre in MAGA circles, championed, for example, by senior advisor at the State Department, Darren Beattie. Outside this, the cases of ISIS, Al Qaeda, the Taliban, and other non-state actors will predominate and direct policy towards both Pakistan and, of course, Afghanistan.

While Central Asian countries have not been noteworthy in policy statements from either Trump's first term or the opening days of the current administration, they constitute the geography where the balancing line between the U.S. and China will be defined. The extent to which Trump defers to Chinese influence in these countries, which have geostrategic importance vis-à-vis energy supplies, will have implications.

Africa

Under the current administration, Africa will move from an aid lens to one of trade. Already, programs under the USAID umbrella are being dismantled. Preferential trade agreements that provided African countries access to the American market could be revised or discarded.

The current administration will build on the Prosper Africa initiative from the first Trump term. This will include trade growth and access for American companies to African markets. It will also involve, more expansively, supply access to what Trump sees as the energy of the future: critical minerals, which relate to the AI industry and beyond.

Most of this falls under the imperative of advancing American prosperity. The administration will probably develop relations with regional countries to play security roles so that the U.S. does not need to overextend its forces on the continent. This will mean de-prioritizing democracy.

Finally, South Africa is seen as a weak link in the BRICS coalition, which President Trump sees as challenging the U.S. dollar's primacy. The administration will continue to target the country until it relents on certain positions, notably its bandwagoning with China.

Other Regions

The global map does not cover two outlining regions as neatly. One is Oceania, which includes Australia, New Zealand, and the Polynesian, Micronesian, and Melanesian islands. U.S. territories and military forces are present here. The U.S. will primarily engage Australia and New Zealand in a way similar to Canada and Europe: It will maintain a security alignment but still situate the relationships transactionally and try to rectify trade imbalances. Through the AUKUS security partnership involving the UK, Australia is already committed to investing in America by acquiring nuclear submarines.

The other region is the Caucasus, which includes Azerbaijan, Armenia, and Georgia, and is enveloped by Russia, Turkey, and Iran. While seemingly remote and small in size, this region has geostrategic relevance as the Trump administration seeks to pull back from American universality, deferring to a balance of power globally and regional security architectures. The Caucasus may prove to be a laboratory for how things elsewhere will develop.

Domestic Policy

For President Trump, domestic and foreign policy go hand in hand. From the MAGA perspective, America has been building international institutions for decades while neglecting the home front. Moreover, the budget allocated has been about—in their eyes—uplifting the world's citizens over everyday Americans. Thus, there is a desire to demonstrate win after win benefiting American citizens. This will also be the policy for evaluating every institution and government body. How do they directly and tangibly benefit American citizens?

Imperatives

Domestic policy is driven by the same underlying America First philosophy and the principles of strength, sovereignty, efficiency, modernization, and traditionalism. Three distinct imperatives—control, irreversibility, and speed—should be noted.

Control

In the Trump 2.5 era, there is a sense that America has lost control of itself. More aptly put, the bureaucracy took control of the executive, rendering the office of the presidency a ceremonial post. With over 2 million civil servants across more than 400 bodies who remain in place through election cycles, it is no surprise that this is a widely held perception. When it comes to regulatory agencies, such as the

Food and Drug Administration, Centers for Disease Control and Prevention, and Environmental Protection Agency, the Trump administration believes that while they have domain expertise, they should not be outside political control.

President Trump and his team see it as an imperative to reinforce direct control of all aspects of the administrative state by the executive. There is pushback on this from Congress, which directly legislates the extent of government programs. A flurry of cases is already in front of the courts; these will litigate the dimensions and limits of executive power. However, this control is the overriding imperative, and all Cabinet officials are dedicated to ensuring direct control to drive policy decisions, including eliminating staff and programs to align with the White House agenda. Time will tell whether this will be successful or whether it will cause damage to the functioning of America, its government, and its economy.

Irreversibility

A second imperative is irreversibility. After the first Trump administration, many changes were reversed through executive orders. Following the experience of Trump, his family, and other associates, who were subject to multiple investigations by the Department of Justice, there is a determination that what they call the 'deep state' cannot return. Thus, the intention across all changes and with all policies is to ensure they are irreversible.

The administration, where possible, will try to eliminate formal bodies and departments rather than merely lessen or shrink them. Employees will be (and have already been) furloughed and their positions eliminated. Regulations will be scrapped, and new projects that would be costly to reverse will be launched.

Speed

In a somewhat Machiavellian way, Trump's absence from politics provided plenty of time for his team to plan how they would exercise power during a second term. And that is precisely what they are doing, as demonstrated in the early innings. The idea is to overwhelm with speed from the outset. That includes frontloading all the changes and new policies that must be implemented.

The notion of speed, however, goes beyond overwhelming the opposition. It has two other aspects. Politically, the Trump administration sees a limited window to achieve its aims. The early cliff is the 2026 midterms. In addition, the Republican primary will begin the following year, 2027, and will also capture political oxygen. With only this term to achieve his aims, Trump has to build and capture momentum before he begins to lose political ground.

The administration also seeks to restore speed to enacting policies and realizing projects. In roughly three years, Donald Trump built his flagship Trump Tower in New York. Whether it is a high-speed rail project, a new manufacturing plant, or an AI initiative, the administration will push accelerated timelines. The best example of this during the first Trump term would be Operation Warp Speed, which, although now maligned by his base, developed the COVID-19 vaccines in record time through a mix of financial incentives, legal guarantees, and waived regulations.

Top Priorities

Beyond the overarching philosophy, principles, and imperatives, the Trump administration is advancing three guiding priorities: borders, energy, and investment. In effect, these priorities serve as drivers for the domestic agenda.

Borders

Securing the border is what Trump sees as the reason he was elected and the primary issue motivating his base, as stated in a number of interviews. Proponents point to a secure border as the basis for sovereignty. An unsecured border also exacerbates the fentanyl crisis in America. Critics contend that this is a smokescreen for a nativist, if not a racist, undertone, and that it is not about illegal immigration or drug trafficking but, in fact, legal immigration.

There are elements of truth to both arguments. The border-related priorities for the Trump team are to stem the flow of illegal migrants as well as to overhaul the legal immigration system. Within the Trump administration, there is a belief that America does not attract the best talent to the country, with legal immigration having become politicized to align with the DEI agenda across the government.

Within the early days of the Trump administration, and with his border czar in place, illegal crossings fell dramatically. Even the initial skirmishes with allies and around tariffs were with the border states of Mexico and Canada. After his appointment, Secretary of Defense Pete Hegseth toured the border and oversaw a military contingent's deployment to reinforce activities. This, however, is not a 100-day priority but will be sustained for four years. It has four components: interdiction, removal, reform, and citizenship.

INTERDICTION

Concerning interdiction, the Trump administration will endeavor to stem the flow of human and drug trafficking to near-zero levels. This will include deploying troops on the border and heightening sea and air patrols on the coasts. It will also involve the completion of and strengthening the border wall. Finally, it will enhance technological monitoring capabilities by incorporating drones, AI, and whatever else is required.

Beyond the physical aspects, the plan is to stop migrants and drugs at the source. All source countries are being pressured to monitor emigration from their borders. Even when interdiction occurs, and asylum cases are being evaluated, as much as possible, the operations are dedicated to keeping migrants off of U.S. soil. This echoes Australia's policies over the last decade, and the facilities of Guantanamo Bay have been expanded for this purpose.

Finally, interdiction is about sending a message that the U.S. border is closed. Evocative images and videos are being released to achieve this effect. Drug traffickers will be made examples of. This is as much about communications for deterrence as it is about physical interception.

Removal

While this may reduce new arrivals, reports have estimated that there are tens of millions of illegal migrants already in the United States. The estimates have varied, but this number may have reached more than 25 million. The idea of mass deportation has never been tested, although, compared to others, the Obama administration achieved the highest number, deporting, on average, almost 400,000 people per year. This rate would remove just over 1.5 million people during Trump's second term.

The Trump administration will follow a similar policy in part. The removal policy will look at removing criminal elements, those with gang affiliations, and migrants with existing deportation orders who have exhausted the legal process. Concurrent with this, however, is the plan to induce the outflow of illegal migrants. This is done by creating a legal 'black hole' for people in the country illegally so that they cannot access public services, travel on interstate transportation, or secure work. Penalties will be increased in workplaces that employ illegal migrants. Furthermore, most migrants granted temporary protection status by executive order or the executive branch will have that status canceled, subjecting their presence to deportation.

Again, the induced migration policy is largely about sending a signal. The idea is to create fear in migrant communities by conveying that deportation might be imminent. The message is if they are forcibly deported—rather than choosing to self-deport—they could be sent to Guantanamo Bay.

In addition, they would be banned from any future entry to the country.

REFORM

Illegal immigration is not the only concern. The Trump administration feels that Americans across classes have been playing second fiddle to both skilled and unskilled immigrants. This creates a market dynamic that lowers wages, disincentivizes the hiring of Americans, and reduces the engagement of American citizens in the economy of tomorrow.

The MAGA movement generally claims that loosely controlled immigration has deleterious social impacts. The contention is it contributes to a housing crisis, overburdens public services, and reduces community cohesiveness. Unsurprisingly, the case of Springfield, Ohio, and Haitian migrants who had moved there became a lightning rod during the campaign, as it played out on the political battlefield.

The Trump administration will create a clearer cap or quota on immigration both as a whole and in specific categories. It will initiate wholesale reform to ensure that only high-wage and high-skilled immigrants get access to the visas listed as such and that there is no abuse of the system. The administration will also encourage more European, Anglophone, and related immigration, as is the case in the provisional refugee program for the Afrikaner population from South Africa.

CITIZENSHIP

The America First philosophy places a value on American citizenship that confers government protection and has intergenerational resonance. Unsurprisingly, the birthright citizenship executive order came in the early days. Whether or not it will stand the test in the courts, there will be a consistent effort to reverse what the MAGA movement sees as the dilution of citizenship today.

This is commensurate with the principle of sovereignty and the protection of that sovereignty, including for citizens abroad. In the eyes of the Trump administration, this is a two-way street. Citizenship needs to be something that cannot simply be attained on a whim. It has to be earned and then held only by people who are genuinely Americans, although what that constitutes is debatable. Where there is a 'fast track,' the Trump administration intends to extract real value from those seeking to immigrate to the United States. This is the impetus behind the "gold card" that may have a price tag of $5 million.

The priority of borders and immigration goes beyond illegal crossings to a much more expansive orientation of new policies.

Energy

The Trump administration prioritizes the potential of America's energy industry, which should not be underestimated. The policy, partly outlined in one of the Trump administration's executive orders, "Unleashing American Energy," will include accelerating approvals, diluting environmental standards, withdrawing from international agreements, and creating incentives, all to enable new projects.

Trump has been speaking about America's energy potential for decades. For the president, oil is an indispensable factor in America's economy. Trump rose to prominence after the recession and inflation crisis of the 1970s, partly driven by the OPEC boycott and rising oil prices. American independence was frequently undermined by wars to safeguard energy resources. Thus, for Trump, energy independence is pivotal for American retrenchment from far-flung adventures and for reducing inflation.

An additional dimension is that energy—in the eyes of the Trump administration—goes beyond oil to include other elements of the supply chain in the industries of tomorrow.

Aligned with the principle of modernization, this signifies that what may be vital inputs into growing and future industries are seen within the same context. This notably includes rare earth minerals.

Approvals

The Trump administration has already rescinded restrictions put in place by the Biden administration, but this is just the beginning. The heart of the plan is to fully unburden all energy and mineral exploration in the U.S. While the appropriate environmental protections will likely remain in place, they may be overridden.

The guiding perspective is not to adhere to regulations but rather to start from zero. Each existing regulation will need to be justified or removed by executive order. The principal factor is how quickly approvals enable a project to proceed from inception to completion.

Many analysts will claim that energy prices will not be allowed to fall too low, as that would then make exploration too costly. This is an incorrect reading, at least on the supply side. The Trump administration wants oil prices to fall to their lowest in decades. To achieve this, they will try to drive down the cost of exploration and the hidden costs of regulation and compliance. Nevertheless, demand conditions could always cause energy prices to rise.

Standards

Today, the energy industry has innumerable standards put in place by government. Over the last two decades, these have coalesced around the environmental, social, and governance (ESG) framing. Much of this has been driven by the climate change agenda. The Trump administration wants to remove any adherence to ESG and anything that modulates energy exploration or industries due to concerns about climate change.

This includes vehicle standards and requirements. Any quota or efficiency requirement for electric vehicles is simply a non-starter. Any standards to remove energy supply to comply with ESG or emission requirements are anticipated to be targeted. The idea is to have a 'non-standard' view of energy supply. The basis is more energy, not conservation.

Agreements

The Trump administration removed itself from the Paris climate accords, echoing a similar action during Trump's first term. As the initial executive orders indicate, domestic concerns will take precedence over international commitments. This is only the beginning. The second Trump administration will systematically review any international accord, commitment, or body to which the United States is a party. It will assess whether or not this engagement restricts domestic energy production. If it does, the U.S. will withdraw and nullify any restrictions that this may impose on the U.S.

From a global competitiveness perspective, the Trump administration will undermine global climate standards and motivate countries to refrain from participating. What would be the point of restricting production if the world's largest economy and energy producer were not participating?

Incentives

The Trump administration's approach to fully mobilizing the private sector to participate in the energy sector will be multifaceted. Most large-scale energy projects take decades to bear fruit, extending beyond Trump's term. In addition, only so much is achievable through executive orders. The right incentives include additional concessions, tax abatements, and potential co-financing that require congressional approval. This is at the top of the agenda for the Trump administration's engagement with Congress.

Investment

To enable American prosperity at the level envisioned by the Trump administration, trillions of dollars of new domestic and foreign investment will be needed. Even before the inauguration, a handful of billionaires and business magnates, most prominent among them SoftBank's Masayoshi Son, descended on Mar-a-Lago to make such commitments (at least on paper). In the administration's early days, the Stargate AI platform was announced to invest up to $500 billion in AI infrastructure.

While these announcements indicate potential inflows, a more systematic strategy is needed. Various components, such as a sovereign wealth fund, tariffs, and access, will be expected to help achieve the desired level of investment. Beyond this, the Trump administration believes that emphasizing its agenda will overall strengthen the American economy and make it an investment destination.

SOVEREIGN WEALTH FUND

President Trump is pushing for the creation of a sovereign wealth fund to invest in the domestic capabilities of the United States, hoping to bring about a centralized and consolidated strategy for directing U.S. investment. Given the immense assets under the federal government's control, creating a sovereign wealth fund is perhaps overdue.

As a funding partner, a sovereign wealth fund would incentivize other partners and attract the largest pools of capital to co-invest in projects. An American sovereign wealth fund could be worth north of $5 trillion, the current value of total federal government assets that have been tangibly documented and are monetizable.

TARIFFS

The Trump administration is leveraging tariffs to try to reinvigorate domestic manufacturing. If American companies produced goods and services within the sovereignty of the United States, they would not be subject to tariffs. Given that the U.S. is the world's largest consumer market, this could create a tremendous incentive to locate manufacturing facilities within the United States. The theory is that a growing U.S. manufacturing base would attract global investors. This would foster a dynamic wherein the most significant investment returns would come from investing in American manufacturing.

While tariffs may help bring investment to the U.S., they could have adverse effects. Risks flagged by economists include inflation due to higher prices and retaliatory measures that create shortages of goods. Stepping back, the investment cycle takes over a decade or more. Thus, the short-term data will only show indicative results and will be the hardest to sustain politically.

ACCESS

The cost of capital for large-scale infrastructure projects and new manufacturing plants is immense. In a hyper-financialized global economy, it makes more sense for investors to pursue returns in financial markets. The White House promises partners, whether SoftBank or others, that plans will be 'fast-tracked,' as outlined in the "America First Investment Policy" executive order.

Thus, a tailored plan will be needed to remove barriers—prohibitive taxes or costly regulations—to projects attracting large investment funds. This would act as an incentive for those seeking to bring capital to the American market. Given this policy, there would be room for abuse and phantom commitments, and the details would be essential to understanding whether this will generate actual returns.

Issues

The Trump administration's agenda is dizzying in scope. This section provides a brief overview of the domestic issues at the forefront. For a more comprehensive understanding, readers should track new emerging issues and note nuances that evolve in the ones detailed in these pages.

Artificial Intelligence

In appointing David Sacks to a role in the White House, the Trump administration has signaled that it wants to be a leader in AI. It sees AI as a national security asset, similar to energy and critical minerals. The Trump administration also sees AI as part of a modernized American economy in the years to come. The one guiding objective is to ensure American AI dominance. This includes attracting investment to bolster the upstream requirements for modern AI, from computing capabilities to data centers. It also includes attracting global talent while cultivating it in America, which will have tension with the priority of immigration reform. The focus of the Biden administration on AI safety will take a backseat. In remarks by the vice president at a summit in France, he indicated the administration's policy shift from AI safety to AI opportunity.

What is yet to be decided is the extent to which the administration will be involved in steering this issue or deferring to private sector leadership, which is already underway. The Stargate AI announcement brought together dominant players, although Elon Musk publicly criticized it. In the coming twelve months, more signature announcements will likely be made on this issue.

Crypto

The Trump administration wants the United States to become the global capital of crypto. It has already reversed the challenging relationship that past administrations had with the industry, whose main players celebrated Trump's election win. During the inauguration week, the Crypto Ball was one of the most well-attended events.

President Trump does not see Bitcoin or other cryptocurrencies as a threat to the U.S. dollar's status as a reserve currency. He sees them as an opportunity for the American economy. Thus, the goal is to locate the facilities of globally pre-eminent companies within the U.S. In addition, the White House is moving to ensure that cryptocurrencies are regulated as securities, although this would exclude meme coins and NFTs, which would be treated as collectibles. Over time, a crypto reserve will be set up, with Bitcoin as the primary holding.

Deregulation

Deregulation is a component across other parts of the domestic agenda, but it is also a stand-alone issue in its own right. The "Unleashing Prosperity through Deregulation" executive order established a 10-for-1 formula. During the first Trump term, the standard was that two resolutions should be removed for each one created. However, the pages of the *Code of Federal Regulations* increased during that period. Whether this administration can achieve a reduction and this lofty ratio remains an open question.

The administration will eliminate regulations it deems costly and political—e.g., DEI-related requirements—and others linked to international rubrics, such as ESG, the SDGs, and various climate standards. Similar to DOGE's focus on workforce reduction, a consolidated list of regulations being cut will be compiled to demonstrate progress.

The overall judicial climate perhaps favors this approach after the landmark Chevron decision in June 2024. In that case, the Supreme Court ruled that government bodies and agencies must closely follow the letter of the existing law and cannot expand or change its scope through expert interpretation. This could also become an obstacle because it partly empowers the judiciary over the executive regarding when and how to apply regulations.

Government Reduction

Another issue is the absolute reduction in the size of the government and its associated workforce. Irrespective of function, the Trump administration seeks to shrink the size of the government and the number of workers. Depending on how it's calculated, between 2 and 3 million people are on the federal payroll. While no formal target has been set, some agencies and bodies are aiming for a 25% reduction.

The steps to this are already underway across the administration. Contingent workers and contractors are being targeted at the outset as they have fewer labor protections. Almost all federal workers have also been given the option to resign proactively with half a year of intended severance. In addition, those who do not return from remote work will be let go. Recent hires on probation have been given termination notices, and pending job offers have been withdrawn. Measures are being taken to avoid systematic layoffs—although this will also occur—and instead induce resignations.

Intelligence Overhaul

Restructuring U.S. intelligence agencies to prevent what the Trump administration would call the 'weaponization of government' is a crucial part of the agenda. This includes ensuring that intelligence agencies are not involved in the unauthorized surveillance of American citizens and scrutinizing any domestic propaganda. There may be proposals to reduce the number of locations where intelligence services are engaged in strengthening opposition movements around the world.

Unlike in the first term, the second Trump administration has appointed stalwarts of the MAGA movement to key positions with the appointment of Tulsi Gabbard, director of national intelligence, and John Ratcliffe, CIA director. They will strive to align the activities of the intelligence agencies with the president's agenda, which means prioritizing the Western hemisphere and protecting American sovereignty. Of course, there will be resistance to change.

Manufacturing

American manufacturing is a fundamental issue in the Trump 2.5 era. While America's manufacturing base has declined over the decades, the administration sees it as vital for the country's future economy and national security. Regardless of industry, the Trump administration has been adamant that it will assist American manufacturing and the employment of Americans in manufacturing.

Tariffs are being used to level the playing field for American domestic producers, notably in the automotive sector. However, for more vital sectors like steel, aluminum, and semiconductors, the plan is also to incentivize the relocation of manufacturing to the United States and proactively drive partnerships to ensure domestic production, even when it is less economically lucrative.

Preventative Health

Incorporating the MAHA (Make America Healthy Again) agenda into the MAGA movement and the appointment of RFK Jr. are fundamental to the Trump administration. MAHA has expanded the base of the Republican Party. There will be a serious plan to overhaul America's supply chains and ensure healthy outcomes as the administration sees them. This will be controversial, as traditional experts may be excluded from the process. It will touch on aspects of food supply and the nature of pharmaceutical medicines. The systematic guidance will mean that all current research grants will be re-evaluated.

RFK Jr. and his team are focused on the country's chronic disease epidemic. They will reevaluate all existing studies to understand the causes of this trend and begin to reorient health policy. An interdepartmental commission has been set up for this purpose. They also have a stated aim to implement radical transparency and disclose any perceived corporate conflicts of interest.

Social Restoration

The Trump administration seeks to return America to the standard of social dynamics two decades ago. This predominantly includes the removal of DEI and the 'T+' in the LGBT+ framing. DEI(A)—the A represents accessibility and is often added to this acronym—is being removed throughout the entire administration. The notion of two genders is also being restored as the baseline, as covered in an officially released Department of Health and Human Services directive. No explicit policy or funding will be used domestically or internationally to advance these two concepts of DEI and gender theory.

The overt preference of DEI programs is to create an environment where all groups feel represented. For the Trump administration, however, these programs are tantamount to reverse discrimination, suppression of merit, and reinforcement of divisions. Removing DEI will mean that race or marginalized status will not be considered in any aspect of recruitment or procurement, and the government will not sponsor alternative cultural programming.

Of course, such a far-reaching position will have collateral impact. For instance, are federal employees allowed to celebrate Martin Luther King Jr. Day, or is that a DEI activity? The White House still commemorated Black History Month in February 2025, and Women's History Month in March 2025, but will it continue the practice with respect to other groups?

While new transgender recruits will be barred from the military, what will the process be for existing officers? In addition, in rolling back protections, there is the real risk that when racism and sexism do surface, the government will be biased against hearing those grievances. Regardless, the administration and the MAGA movement feel the pendulum has swung too far one way on this issue and that a course correction is required.

Principles and Policies

Taxes

Taxes were a consistent theme of Trump's campaign. His administration's approach is twofold: reducing taxes and complexity. The Trump administration would prefer to reduce income tax to zero and throw out the IRS rulebook. In practice, it is expected to settle—in concert with Congress—to drastically reduce corporate and personal income tax and simplify the tax code. Campaign promises, including eliminating taxes on tips and social security, will also be put into practice.

One of the administration's executive orders proposes creating an ERS to collect tariff revenue. Before the introduction of a federal income tax in 1913, this was how the U.S. government was primarily funded. While that would be improbable today, this administration might explore a seismic shift in how the government collects revenue.

Voter Transparency

While Trump won in 2024, he and his team still do not believe the 2020 elections were fair and secure. Thus, there is likely to be a nationwide initiative to promote voting transparency and drive new requirements for voter identification. The federal government has oversight over certain aspects of voting, even though each state determines its procedures.

In the early days of this term, the president floated the idea of making disaster aid to California conditional on changing voter identification laws. Republican lawmakers have also proposed using artificial intelligence to investigate the integrity of voter rolls. This issue may become a point of contention ahead of the 2026 midterm elections.

Override

Plans are easy to make but hard to execute. It is even harder to follow through when circumstances overtake the moment. This situation arose during the first Trump term when the COVID-19 pandemic dominated every aspect of life in the final year of the presidency.

It is not just world events that may lead to deviations from the various principles and policies outlined in this chapter. At times, the DC establishment, even within Republican circles, will require horse-trading to break the gridlock. Similarly, President Trump will look to make the art of the deal in foreign relations.

There is an override function that will fit the politics of the moment. What is apparent is that Trump's base is willing to follow him wherever he goes in political battle, with the recognition that his direction is vital to achieving fundamental aims.

Art of the DC

In its second term, the Trump administration will maneuver as much as possible through the White House by promulgating executive orders. Unlike in the first term, when President Trump signed executive orders at a rate of many previous presidents, he has increased the pace this time around. Still, only so much can be done at the presidential level.

Congress has the power of the purse, according to the Constitution. In addition to changes in the budget, to establish or, conversely, disband government bodies or agencies, President Trump will need alignment with Congress. There are initiatives that the administration would desire to have as its legacy, whether in infrastructure, artificial intelligence, or space travel. This would also necessitate working in a bipartisan way with legislators.

This could come to a head around the end of April 2025, when a congressional deadline triggers automatic government funding cuts. Regardless, this will recur annually during the budget cycle. During these moments, the White House may back down from certain positions.

Too many concessions will raise tensions within the MAGA movement. However, by working hand-in-hand with the president on his nominations, Senate Majority Leader John Thune has earned goodwill. As long as the philosophy of America First is followed, compromises will follow in legislation.

Art of the Deal

During the 2024 political campaign, Trump very authoritatively removed hardline abortion stances from the platform. Ahead of the Republican National Convention, his team effectively locked delegates in a room and did not let them emerge until they signed the GOP platform they had drafted. That platform removed distinct pro-life provisions that had been mainstays of the party. It demonstrated Trump's politically expedient decisions to ensure success, even if otherwise, such a position would have been considered sacrilegious in the party.

In pursuing the art of the deal beyond party politics, Trump will turn to two constituencies: the voting population and foreign leaders. By positioning the Republican platform carefully on social issues, Trump looked to build a broad-based coalition. Ensuring enough interests are met across constituencies—even if they were not traditional conservatives—brought about an electoral mandate. The same stance is presumed ahead of the 2026 midterms. If there is a policy that is championed by his team but potentially causes a loss of votes, Trump may drop it from the agenda.

In more tangible deal-making, Trump will seek as many agreements as possible with America's rivals. In these cases, there will need to be trade-offs. For example, to achieve the right alignment with China, the latter would have to partially acquiesce to tariffs.

With only four years in power, Trump will be in a deal-making mode. Escalation and aggressive postures will be sudden, frequent, and almost hyperbolic, yet the climb-down will be as quick.

There are plenty of trade-offs that the administration will be weighing; trying to follow a recipe rather than a sense of America First will cause observers to misevaluate where things are heading. Trump 2.5 is about irreversibly changing the course of the American economy and political system.

World Events

In the first term, the COVID-19 pandemic derailed the Trump administration's agenda and was a factor in his loss in the election later that year. While a pandemic is unlikely to have the same effect during the second term, natural disasters and war are challenges with the potential to override the agenda. That is why President Trump will strive to calm tensions with rivals in China and Russia and minimize the possibility of direct confrontation with Iran and North Korea.

On a smaller scale, the true threat is not one cataclysmic event but a series of ongoing crises and flare-ups. The Trump administration's aggressive actions may precipitate this. Domestically, DOGE could alienate multiple constituencies, precipitating opposition and potential work stoppages or other challenges to the operation of critical infrastructure. Internationally, pressures may lead to political pushback from other countries and even the emergence of sub-state threats to American interests.

How the administration compartmentalizes these challenges and multi-tasks its political priorities to ensure sustained momentum will be instructive. Unlike in the first term, the administration appears much more consolidated and cohesive, and most appointees are firmly part of the MAGA movement.

IV

PEOPLE AND POSITIONS

For many readers, this section will be the most engaging. At the same time, others may use it as a reference tool to return to when appropriate. Given the dynamic situation, the individuals listed here may change in terms of roles and responsibilities. Other figures not included in this chapter might emerge over time. The website associated with this publication—TrumpPrimer.com—will continue to have updates on the most salient developments where possible.

It should be noted that this chapter does not cover the judiciary, including justices who may be partial to the president and his agenda. The U.S. Supreme Court will decide various disputes in the next four years, particularly on the limits of executive power. However, this primer treats the judicial branch as independent of politics despite the biases of individual justices.

That being said, it is worth keeping in mind that the highest court is right-leaning and has been appointed mainly by Republican presidents. It will have a conservative and originalist disposition and could side with the Trump administration. At the appellate level, there is a relatively even split between Democrat- and Republican-appointed judges. There is a far greater share of Democrat-appointed judges at the district level. At this lowest level, plaintiffs can target a jurisdiction when filing a case so that a particular judge receives it. Thus, as disputes emerge, it will often seem initially that the tide is against the administration, but this may balance out as cases find their way through the courts.

First Family

The Trump family is integrated into President Trump's decision-making. They have been in his inner circle and, at various stages, at the forefront and center of his political campaigns. While the Trump administration has a broad political apparatus, the influence of the First Family should not be underestimated.

- **Barron Trump**—The president's youngest child is an undergraduate student at New York University. He was involved in the 2024 campaign, informing the podcast strategy targeting Gen Z.
- **Bettina Anderson**—The girlfriend of Donald Trump Jr. is a regular on the Miami social scene. Unlike other partners, she does not have a substantive political role.
- **Donald Trump Jr.**—The eldest son of President Trump co-leads the Trump Organization with his brother Eric Trump. He is one of three children from President Trump's marriage to the late Ivana Trump. Don Jr., as he is known, has been outspoken politically and hosts a podcast. He took personal credit for JD Vance's selection as the vice presidential candidate.
- **Eric Trump**—The youngest of three children from Donald and Ivana Trump's marriage co-leads the Trump Organization with his brother, Donald Trump Jr. While less of a political force than his older brother, he has guided the family's recent forays into the crypto industry.
- **Ivanka Trump**—The eldest Trump daughter was a fashion fixture in New York before the first term. Then, she

played a high-profile role in the White House as an advisor to the president, primarily on women's empowerment. During the second term, she does not have a political role.

- **Jared Kushner**—The president's son-in-law married Ivanka Trump in 2009, and they have three children together. After playing a lead role in Middle East policy during Donald Trump's first term, he has stepped back to devote his time to growing business interests. Notably, Saudi Arabia has given his fund, Affinity Partners, deep financial backing.

- **Kai Trump**—The eldest granddaughter of Donald Trump has entered the social media limelight. She is an avid golfer and will attend the University of Miami in the fall. She is the daughter of Donald Trump Jr. and his ex-wife Vanessa Trump.

- **Lara Trump**—The wife of Eric Trump played a monumental role in the 2024 presidential campaign as the co-chair of the Republican National Committee. She has now returned to her television roots. She and Eric have two children together.

- **Melania Trump**—Donald Trump's current wife is originally from Slovenia. She was a model who moved to New York at age 26 in 1996 and met Donald Trump two years later. While they dated intermittently for several years, by the early 2000s, they had settled into a relationship and married in 2005. She continued to model, but that took a back seat when she gave birth to her son, Barron Trump, in 2006.

While independently minded and sometimes distant, Melania has played a pivotal role by Trump's side on the campaign trail and in the White House. Look for her to be active on a few fronts and launch initiatives building on her "Be Best" movement from the first term.

- **Michael Boulos**—The newest family member, so to speak, married Tiffany Trump in 2022. Originally Lebanese from Nigeria, he met Tiffany in 2018. While he is involved in a family business with his father, Massad Boulos, little more is known about his business background.
- **Tiffany Trump**—The only child from Donald Trump's marriage to Marla Maples, she has mostly stayed out of the political spotlight. She spoke at the Republican National Convention in 2024. Now, expecting her first child with her husband, she is not looking to play an immediate role in the administration.

Although more distant relatives are not listed here, they may be part of news cycles. One is Marla Maples, Trump's ex-wife, who is a big advocate of the MAHA agenda, and the other is his niece, Mary Trump, who has become a critic of her uncle.

Presidential Staff

President Trump has a close-knit team of staff in the White House to carry out his agenda. A number of them have worked in politics alongside the president for a decade. Compared to the first term, this will translate to fewer leaks and more coordinated messaging.

- **JD Vance | Vice President**—Vance is the other elected member of the executive branch and can only be removed by the Senate through an impeachment process. He has his own office and staff in the West Wing and is part of the Cabinet. The role the vice president plays depends on the administration. Dick Cheney was the last vice president who appeared to be as instrumental in White House policy. Without a clear portfolio, the position can become a ceremonial one. Of course, in the case of tragedy or scandal, the vice president would step into the presidency. The last to do so was Gerald Ford after the resignation of President Richard Nixon in 1974.

Vance is just 40 years of age and only entered elected politics in 2022 when he ran for and won a seat as the senator for Ohio. His story, overall, was captured in his bestselling memoir, *Hillbilly Elegy*, which was also turned into a movie in 2020. At the time, Vance emerged as an interpreter in the public eye for the so-called "forgotten men and women" in middle America who constituted part of the MAGA movement and to whom Trump often referred.

After high school, Vance joined the Marine Corps, where he served as a military journalist in the initial years after the invasion of Iraq in 2003, following which he left to go to college. He eventually attended Yale Law School, where he met his future wife, Usha Chilukuri, with whom he has three children. Vivek Ramaswamy was in the same class. After law school, he clerked for a federal judge and briefly worked in Senator Cornyn's office on the Hill. However, he was drawn to venture capital and joined one of Peter Thiel's firms before setting out on his own. Thiel remained a backer of his, including when he decided to run for the Senate.

Politically, Vance sharply criticized Trump in 2016 but later changed his views. By the time Trump chose him for the Republican ticket, he was already one of the core voices in the MAGA movement. During the campaign and since assuming office, he has been a constant presence on the Sunday talk show circuit. His combative but eloquent style has earned supporters on the Republican side and detractors among those who oppose his platform.

Vance represents a conduit for the techno-political wing into the White House, and his existing relationships in

Silicon Valley have informed the selection of personnel across the administration. Yet, his background, having grown up in poverty in a household with a broken family, drug addiction, and abuse, endears him to the populist base of the MAGA movement. In current polling for the 2028 election, Vance leads the way on the Republican side. That being said, President Trump has said he has no chosen successor.

With so many personalities in the current White House, Vance may be crowded out by others like Elon Musk and RFK Jr. However, he is quickly building a platform of his own. In the early days of the administration his role has been as a top communications surrogate, alternative diplomat-in-chief, and convenor on technology. This set of responsibilities will likely sharpen in the coming twelve months, especially as certain issues evolve. In all cases, he is a critical part of the administration and should not be underestimated or forgotten amidst all the noise.

- **Alex Wong | Principal Deputy National Security Advisor**—Wong works across the portfolio with Mike Waltz, the national security advisor. He has worked in various positions in Washington DC over two decades and served in the State Department during the first Trump administration.

- **Alina Habba | Counselor**—Habba was in a role as a communications surrogate but has since been appointed as an interim U.S. attorney. In 2019, she became acquainted with Trump at his golf club in Bedminster and has served as his lawyer in civil cases.

- **Andy Baker | National Security Advisor to the Vice President**—Baker is one of JD Vance's closest advisors. He was a foreign service officer who joined Vance's staff when Vance was in the Senate.

People and Positions 99

- **Ben Moss | Director of the Domestic Council for the Vice President**—Moss is a lawyer who served as counsel in Vance's Senate office. He earlier worked in the Texas office of the law firm Vinson & Elkins.

- **Brian Hughes | Deputy National Security Advisor for Communications**—Hughes is effectively the spokesperson for the National Security Council, a role that Obama appointee Ben Rhodes once held. He also served as a transition spokesperson for the Trump campaign.

- **Dan Scavino | Principal Deputy Chief of Staff**—Scavino is a steady hand for the president. He has been involved in politics since 2015 and served in the first Trump administration. In the 2000s, he started his career in Trump's orbit as the general manager of one of his golf courses.

- **David Sacks | AI & Crypto Czar**—Sacks heads the Presidential Council of Advisors on Science & Technology in addition to overseeing policy for the artificial intelligence and crypto industries. He founded Craft Ventures and is part of the South African 'PayPal mafia' alongside Peter Thiel and Elon Musk. In 2024, he was an early benefactor of the Trump campaign in Silicon Valley.

- **David Warrington | Counsel**—Warrington is the president's lead legal advisor. He represented Trump on a variety of fronts during the 2024 campaign. He was a partner in the law firm of Harmeet Dhillon and a legal counsel for Republicans prosecuted by the Department of Justice in recent years.

- **Devin Nunes | Chair of the President's Intelligence Advisory Board**—Nunes is a close confidant of the president and is relied upon to provide a neutral perspective in this voluntary position. During his first term as a congressman, he was essential in unveiling the origins of the Russia investigation. Subsequently, he became the CEO of TMTG, which he still leads.

- **Elon Musk | Head of the Department of Government Efficiency (DOGE)**—Musk is arguably the second most powerful person in the administration. He unofficially leads DOGE, formerly the Office of Digital Services, which was established by an executive order during the Obama administration. His objective until July 4, 2026, is to cut up to $2 trillion of government spending. He is doing so agency by agency with a small team of engineers and personnel in coordination with the White House. It is unclear how conflicts of interest will be resolved, given that Musk's companies receive billions of dollars in annual contracts, subsidies, and concessions and are regulated by the same agencies.

  Musk is one of the most established technologists of his time and is almost single-handedly responsible for driving the American return to space travel. His company, Tesla, is now one of the largest automobile companies in the world and is on its way to global leadership in robotics. Neuralink is at the forefront of brain-computer interfaces. While X (formerly known as Twitter) is the public square and a salient platform for Trump officials, it is X.AI that may end up the predominant entity. Musk has rivalries with technologists Bill Gates and Sam Altman. While overseeing DOGE today, he will have a second act in the administration regarding space travel.

- **Hayley Harrison | Chief of Staff to the First Lady**—Harrison is the closest aide to Melania Trump in the East Wing. She served in the first administration and continued to work for the First Lady in the intervening years at Mar-a-Lago.

- **Jacob Reses | Chief of Staff to the Vice President**—Reses served in the same role for the vice president when he was a senator. Before this, he worked for Senators Hawley and Cruz. He had earlier worked for the conservative news outlet *The Daily Caller*.

- **James Blair | Deputy Chief of Staff for Legislative Affairs**—Blair was a close member of the president's campaign team. He has a background in political consulting and was also a former staffer in Governor DeSantis's office.
- **James Braid | Director of Office of Legislative Affairs**—Braid worked for the Office of Management and Budget during the first Trump administration and worked on the Hill as a staffer in JD Vance's office.
- **Jim Goyer | Director of the Office of Public Liaison**—Goyer was deputy director during the first Trump term. He most recently worked at Goldman Sachs and has held other political roles within the Republican establishment.
- **Karoline Leavitt | Press Secretary**—Leavitt is the administration's spokesperson and one of its youngest members. She worked briefly in the White House during Trump's first term and has held various communications roles in politics. Leavitt ran for Congress in 2022 but did not win a seat.
- **Kevin Hassett | Director of the National Economic Council**—Hassett is a well-known economist based in Washington, DC, who has served multiple presidential administrations. During the first Trump term, he served as chair of the Council of Economic Advisors. His role this time around is more policy-oriented.
- **Lea Bardon | Director of Cabinet Affairs**—Bardon is supporting the cabinet secretary. She worked at the MAGA-linked America First Policy Institute and on Trump's presidential campaigns.

- **Matt Brasseaux | Director of Political Affairs**—Brasseaux has a long history within Republican Party institutions, which will serve him well in this role as effectively their conduit into the White House. He has worked across positions with the RNC.

- **Mike Waltz | National Security Advisor**—Waltz is part of a close circle of trusted advisors to the president who will spearhead global negotiations. He is a three-term congressman, business executive, and four-time Bronze Star recipient.

- **Peter Navarro | Senior Counselor for Trade**—Navarro is a trusted aide to Trump and went to prison for contempt of Congress for refusing to testify in one of the probes against the president. A former Democrat, Navarro is a proponent of 'fair trade,' favoring protectionist measures when there are trade imbalances. He has written a number of books on the America-China dynamic.

- **Richard Grenell | Envoy for Special Missions**—Grenell is a close aide to President Trump and effectively serves as his 'utility' man, similar to the first term. He served as Ambassador to Germany before becoming a special envoy to the Balkans and then acting director of national intelligence. He has been involved in political roles within the Republican Party for over two decades.

- **Ross Worthington | Director of Speechwriting Office**—Worthington helped draft the speech that President Trump delivered near the Capitol on January 6, 2021. During the 2024 campaign, he infused in-depth policy perspectives into Trump's remarks. He is considered another confidante of the president. Before joining Trump's side, he was an aide to former Speaker of the House Newt Gingrich.

- **Sergio Gor | Director of Presidential Personnel**—Gor coordinates political appointments and is one of the most crucial members of the administration. He worked as a staffer for nearly a decade for Senator Rand Paul and, prior to that, for multiple offices in the House.

- **Stephen Miller | Deputy Chief of Staff for Policy**—Miller is the administration's lead thinker on immigration policy. He served in the first Trump White House and was a lightning rod for the media. Prior to this, he worked on the Hill as a congressional staffer. His role continues to grow, and together with his wife, Katie Miller, has become a key interlocutor within Washington, DC.

- **Steven Cheung | Director of Communications**—Cheung is the physically domineering voice of the administration. He helps shape the content on the well-followed Rapid Response account on X. He was the spokesperson for the 2024 presidential campaign and also served in the White House during Trump's first term.

- **Susie Wiles | Chief of Staff**—Wiles is considered to be the glue of the current White House and played a similar role on the campaign trail. She was influential in the cabinet appointments process and maintained discipline in the administration's early days. Wiles has an extensive resume, going back to the Reagan administration. She served on the first Trump Campaign in 2016 and became CEO of the Save America PAC in 2021.

- **Taylor Budowich | Deputy Chief of Staff for Cabinet Affairs and Communications**—Budowich is part of the president's close-knit communications team. He joined the Trump operation when the president sought re-election in 2019. Budowich previously worked for an organization linked to the Tea Party.

- **Thomas Homan | Border Czar**—Homan is the spokesperson and point person for the White House's crackdown on illegal immigration. He started his career as a police officer and soon joined the federal government as a border agent. He rose through the ranks during the Obama administration and was appointed by Trump to head Immigration and Customs Enforcement (ICE) during his first term. In the intervening years, he became increasingly vocal in the media on border enforcement.

- **Vince Haley | Director of the Domestic Policy Council**—Haley understands President Trump as well as anyone. He served as the lead speechwriter during Trump's first term. Before joining the Trump campaign in 2016, he was a close aide to former Speaker of the House Newt Gingrich.

- **Will Scharf | Staff Secretary**—Scharf is a subtly influential White House member responsible for the inflow and outflow of what appears on the president's desk. He played a role in Missouri politics and launched an unsuccessful run for attorney general. He worked on the confirmation process of Supreme Court justices during Trump's first term as an outside advisor.

Countless others with specialized roles could be mentioned. These include, for example, General Keith Kellogg (envoy to Ukraine) and Steve Witkoff (envoy to the Middle East). Witkoff, a close friend of the president, is involved in matters beyond his original file.

Cabinet and Agencies

The president's team was prepared early with nominees for most positions. In addition to the cabinet and agency appointments, the transition team had also prepared lists of other political appointees to serve within the various departments. Most of these appointments have been announced but are not covered here.

People and Positions

Cabinet

The following appointments require Senate approval. In addition to these positions, the vice president and chief of staff are also part of the Cabinet.

- **Brooke Rollins | Secretary of Agriculture**—Rollins has an expansive reach within the Trump administration after serving as the founding CEO of the America First Policy Institute. She worked as policy director in the first Trump White House and got her political start in a similar role in Texas Governor Rick Perry's office. As Agriculture secretary, she is cutting back on regulations but may sometimes diverge from the MAHA agenda on food supply. For now, she is working closely with RFK Jr.

- **Chris Wright | Secretary of Energy**—Wright is an energy entrepreneur and executive who will bring that experience to his new role. He founded a fracking company and sat on the board of a nuclear reactor enterprise. As Energy secretary, he is removing climate-related restrictions wherever possible.

- **Doug Burgum | Secretary of Interior**—Burgum, a two-term governor of North Dakota, was a potential running mate for Donald Trump in 2024. Before becoming governor, he founded and led a venture capital firm, Arthur Ventures. As Interior secretary, he is working closely with the energy secretary to unlock oil and gas exploration.

- **Doug Collins | Secretary of Veterans Affairs (VA)**—Collins is a former Georgia congressman and Air Force veteran who ran unsuccessfully for the Senate in 2020. He subsequently served as Trump's legal counsel. As VA secretary, he is aligning with the administration's agenda to create more efficiency in the department.

- **Elise Stefanik (withdrawn) | Ambassador to the United Nations (UN)**—Stefanik became the fourth-highest-ranking Republican member of the House of Representatives and the youngest woman elected to Congress at 30. Her appointment was withdrawn at the last minute due to concerns over the GOP's narrow majority in the House.

- **Howard Lutnick | Secretary of Commerce**—Lutnick was co-chair of Trump's transition team in 2024, and his relationship with the president goes back decades. He heads the financial firm Cantor Fitzgerald and was CEO when it lost 658 of its employees in the 9/11 attacks. As Commerce secretary, he approves of and will help carry out the White House's tariff policies.

- **Jamieson Greer | U.S. Trade Representative (USTR)**—Greer was chief of staff to the previous USTR in the first Trump administration. Before and after, he served as a private lawyer. As USTR, he is responsible for closing the $1 trillion trade deficit.

- **John Ratcliffe | Director of the Central Intelligence Agency (CIA)**—Ratcliffe was a political appointee of the George W. Bush administration. He also co-led a law firm with Bush-era Attorney General John Ashcroft. Ratcliffe worked as a member of Congress to defend then-President Trump against impeachment and later became acting director of national intelligence. As CIA director, he is expected to bring reform to the agency.

- **Kelly Loeffler | Administrator of the Small Business Administration (SBA)**—Loeffler, a corporate executive, was appointed to the Georgia Senate in 2020 and ran against the Trump-preferred candidate, Doug Collins, that same year. After her election loss, she returned to private business and became a fundraiser for Trump's 2024 campaign. As SBA administrator, she is focusing on domestic manufacturing.

- **Kristi Noem | Secretary of Homeland Security**—Noem was the governor of South Dakota from 2019 until she joined the Cabinet in 2025. Before that, she was a state representative and then a congresswoman. A series of personal controversies undermined her prospects as a potential running mate for Trump. As Homeland Security secretary, she is working closely with the border czar to enforce a strict anti-migration policy.

- **Lee Zeldin | Administrator of the Environmental Protection Agency (EPA)**—Zeldin was a four-term congressman who led the red wave in New York in the 2022 midterm elections to much Republican fanfare. Before entering government, he was a private lawyer who ran unsuccessfully for the New York governor position in 2022. As EPA administrator, he is narrowing the agency's focus from climate change to air and water quality.

- **Linda McMahon | Secretary of Education**—McMahon served in the first administration, heading the SBA, and was a co-chair of the 2024 transition team with Howard Lutnick. She built World Wrestling Entertainment (WWE) with her then-husband, Vince McMahon, over three decades. As Education secretary, she is helping the administration effectively hollow out the department.

- **Lori Chavez-DeRemer | Secretary of Labor**—Chavez-DeRemer most recently served in the House following a tenure as mayor of a small town in Oregon. As a congresswoman, she took pro-union positions. As Labor secretary, she is a bridge to a new plank of the Republican base—workers.

- **Marco Rubio | Secretary of State**—Rubio serves as the acting administrator of USAID in addition to his regular duties as head of the State Department. He served first in the Florida House before running for and winning one of Florida's two Senate seats in 2010. He was considered a front-runner in the 2016 presidential race, fading ultimately due to the rise of Trump. As secretary of state, he is promoting the peace-through-strength formula as America's lead diplomat while also navigating the off-the-cuff deal-making positions set forth by the president.

- **Michael Kratsios | Director of the Office of Science and Technology Policy (OSTP)**—Kratsios served as the chief technology officer of the first Trump White House. Early in his career, he was Peter Thiel's chief of staff. He was most recently part of the executive leadership team at Scale AI, an AI company. As OSTP director, he is expected to work closely with David Sacks to ensure American dominance in AI.

- **Pam Bondi | Attorney General**—Bondi was an early backer of Donald Trump and worked as a lawyer to defend him in the first impeachment process in 2019. Bondi began her career as a prosecutor before becoming Florida's attorney general. She has also operated a private practice. She, alongside her deputy, Todd Blanche, will work to overhaul the Department of Justice to remove what the administration sees as politicization.

- **Pete Hegseth | Secretary of Defense**—Hegseth was one of President Trump's unorthodox appointments. He most recently served as a television co-host on Fox News. He is a veterans advocate, leading initiatives and organizations for that purpose. Having served in Iraq and Afghanistan, he brings a unique perspective to the position. As defense secretary, he is working with DOGE to streamline the Pentagon and focus on "warfighting."

- **Robert F. Kennedy Jr. | Secretary of Health and Human Services (HHS)**—RFK Jr is a central coalition partner who moved Trump's re-election past the line. He also brings the MAHA movement that includes former Democrats to Trump's side. RFK Jr. has a history of environmental and health advocacy, founding organizations with that purpose. He has initiated lawsuits—as a lawyer himself—and written a number of books that outline his views. His positions have been closely scrutinized—and condemned; particularly on vaccine hesitancy. As HHS secretary, he is moving the agency from reactive to preventative health care and will attempt to remove corporate influence in aspects of the department.

- **Russell Vought | Director of the Office of Management and Budget (OMB)**—Vought was the OMB director during the first Trump administration. After 2020, he worked in Washington, DC, with policy organizations, including Heritage Action and on the Hill. As OMB director, he is taking an aggressive posture in monitoring all government spending.

- **Scott Bessent | Secretary of the Treasury**—Bessent is the highest-ranking gay official in U.S. history. While a past fundraiser for Trump, he also had a deep association with George Soros, heading his investment fund. He was involved in one of the most famous trades of all time, shorting the British pound. He most recently led a hedge fund he co-founded. As Treasury secretary, he is concentrating, in his words, on lowering treasury yields to reduce the cost of borrowing.

- **Scott Turner | Secretary of Housing and Urban Development (HUD)**—Turner is a former NFL player turned Texas state representative. He joined the first Trump White House to oversee the opportunity zones initiative. He also has varied business interests. As HUD secretary, he is concentrating on lowering the cost of housing and increasing supply.

- **Sean Duffy | Secretary of Transportation**—Duffy rose to prominence as a reality TV star in the 1990s and later pursued a legal career, becoming a district attorney in Wisconsin. He was elected to the U.S. House of Representatives but resigned to become a lobbyist. As

Transportation secretary, he faced his first challenge with a dramatic airline crash in Washington, DC. He is enforcing standards across the board and modernizing the government's transportation management.

- **Stephen Miran | Chairman of the Council of Economic Advisors**—Miran was a financial analyst and economist before briefly joining the Treasury Department at the tail end of the first Trump administration. He has written extensively criticizing the Federal Reserve for alleged inflationary policies. As the Council chairman, he will work closely with others in the White House to monitor inflation and guide thinking concerning tariffs.

- **Tulsi Gabbard | Director of National Intelligence (DNI)**—Gabbard ran for the Democratic presidential nomination in 2020 but then left the party. She eventually became a Republican in 2024 and endorsed Donald Trump. Prior to that, she was a four-term congresswoman. Due to her anti-war bent and skepticism of what she terms the 'deep state,' she has a loyal base within MAGA circles. While formerly close to Bernie Sanders, that relationship splintered. She is a lieutenant colonel in the Hawaii National Guard. As DNI, she is expected to be critical of the intelligence establishment and oversee agency reform.

These appointments were almost all confirmed within two months of the inauguration, showing incredible efficiency and coordination between the Trump White House and the Senate.

Agencies and Bodies

The government's agencies, commissions, and bodies are essential to the Trump 2.5 agenda. The White House has moved to ensure there are acting heads wherever possible. However, the administration has already nominated candidates—where Senate approval is required—and made direct appointments where they are not. At the time of publication, some have yet to be confirmed by the Senate or are serving in an acting capacity. They are denoted as 'nominee' below.

- **Andrew N. Ferguson | Chair of the Federal Trade Commission**—Ferguson was appointed chair in January 2025 by President Trump and had been appointed as a commissioner by then-President Joe Biden. He was previously a private lawyer and then the solicitor general of Virginia. As FTC chair, he will have a challenge navigating the anti- and pro-Silicon Valley wings of the new Republican Party base.

- **Billy Long (nominee) | Commissioner of the Internal Revenue Service (IRS)**—Long is a six-term congressman from Missouri who most recently worked for private companies applying for increased tax credits. While in the House, he had called for the IRS to be abolished. As IRS commissioner, he will be tasked with streamlining the tax code.

- **Brendan Carr | Chair of the Federal Communications Commission (FCC)**—Carr was a practicing private lawyer before joining the FCC as counsel. He was appointed commissioner during the first Trump term. As chairman, he is driving policy to enable expanded spectrum access and reduce what is seen as the influence of the major networks.

- **Brent Bozell (withdrawn) | Chief Executive Officer of the United States Agency for Global Media (USAGM)**—Bozell is a conservative activist and media critic. He comes from the conservative family of William F. Buckley. Nearly four decades ago, he founded Media Research Center, a media watchdog on the right. His nomination was withdrawn, and his name was instead put forward for ambassador to South Africa.

- **Bryan Bedford (nominee) | Administrator of Federal Aviation Authority (FAA)**—Bedford is an experienced airline executive. He is also a certified pilot. Over the last 25 years, he has been at the helm of Republic Airways, a regional carrier that operates flights for other airlines. As FAA administrator, he is expected to improve the agency's performance and modernize its approach.
- **Chance Saltzman | Chief of Space Operations (CSO)**—Gen. Saltzman was appointed by then-President Biden in 2022. He is a career Air Force officer who joined the recently-created Space Force in 2020. He has experience across aerospace and missile programs. As CSO, he will ensure American military competitiveness in space and support the American Iron Dome project, in line with the administration's agenda.
- **Daniel Driscoll | Secretary of the Army**—Driscoll was a classmate of JD Vance and Jake Sullivan at Yale Law School and served as a platoon leader in the U.S. Army. He has had a varied business career, mainly in finance and technology. He unsuccessfully ran for Congress in 2020. He will improve force readiness as Army secretary and align closely with the defense secretary.
- **David Weldon (withdrawn) | Director of the Centers for Disease Control and Prevention (CDC)**—Weldon is a former eight-term Florida congressman and practicing physician. After retiring from Congress, he ran for Senate and tried to return to the House, but both attempts were unsuccessful. His nomination for CDC director was withdrawn in part due to his skeptical perspective to existing vaccine policy, with the acting director, Susan Monarez named in his place.
- **Dean John Sauer (nominee) | Solicitor General**—Sauer is a prolific legal professional, with a career spanning clerking at the Supreme Court to last year arguing

successfully on the office of the president's immunity on behalf of Trump in front of the same court. He began his career in private practice and eventually became solicitor-general of Missouri and then deputy attorney general. As solicitor general, he will vigorously defend the administration's moves and positions.

- **Janette Nesheiwat (nominee) | U.S. Surgeon General**—Nesheiwat completed her residency in 2009 and has worked for an urgent-care medical company in New York and as a medical correspondent on Fox News. One of her sisters, Julia Nesheiwat, is a former government advisor married to NSA Michael Waltz. Her other sister, Jaclyn Stapp, is married to the lead singer of Creed. As surgeon general, Nesheiwat is not anticipated to have a policy role but instead to be the lead health spokesperson. She will complement the work of RFK Jr. and Mehmet Oz.

- **Jared Isaacman (nominee) | Administrator of NASA**—Isaacman is a qualified military jet pilot and one of the most recognized individuals in the space industry. He led the inaugural fully private human spaceflight in 2021 and returned to space in 2024. One of his companies runs a fleet of private military aircraft, while another he founded at the age of 16 trades on the New York Stock Exchange. As NASA administrator, he will push an innovation viewpoint and further involve the private sector.

- **Jay Bhattacharya | Director of the National Institutes of Health (NIH)**—Bhattacharya emerged as one of the pronounced critics of the COVID-19 response and co-authored the Barrington Declaration. He is a professor at Stanford University and is well-published in scientific journals. He is a strict defender of what he calls scientific freedom. As NIH director, he will facilitate an overhaul of the over $30 billion in annual grants.

- **Joseph Kent (nominee) | Director of the National Counterterrorism Center (NCTC)**—Kent joined the army at 18 and left in 2018 to join the CIA. After his wife, also serving, was killed in a bombing in Syria, he resigned from government service and eventually ran for Congress unsuccessfully in 2022 and 2024, campaigning against 'endless wars.' As NCTC director, he will work to promote an America-first orientation and reduce what the administration sees as remote missions.

- **John Daniel "Razin" Caine (nominee) | Chairman of the Joint Chiefs of Staff (CJCS)**—Lieutenant General Caine (ret.) was nominated by the president to replace General Charles Q. Brown, who himself had succeeded Trump adversary Mark Milley in 2023. He has held multiple roles in the military and executive branch over three decades, beginning his career in the Air Force. More recently, he was an associate director at the CIA until the end of 2024, when he left the government to take on advisory roles with a small group of venture capital firms, including one linked to the Kushner family. As CJCS, he is expected to be responsible for carrying out President Trump's orders without hesitation and delay, unlike his predecessors during the first term.

- **John Phelan | Secretary of the Navy**—Phelan is one of the few military appointments by the administration not to have served. He is an investment manager who primarily served technologist Michael Dell, generating outsized returns over two decades. He was a prolific fundraiser for the Trump campaign in 2024. As Navy secretary, he will look to streamline business operations within its $200 billion annual spend and accelerate shipbuilding.

- **Kari Lake | Director of Voice of America (VOA)**—Lake ran unsuccessfully for governor of Arizona in 2022 and senator in 2024. This was after a career in local media, where she became more forthright about her political positions in later years. She is considered a polarizing figure but has been a firm backer of President Trump. As the VOA director, she will work to narrow what the MAGA movement sees as political and potentially dismantle the network. Her appointment appears to require approval by a bipartisan advisory board, depending on what process is followed.

- **Kashyap Patel | Director of the Federal Bureau of Investigation (FBI)**—Patel served as chief of staff to the defense secretary in the latter days of Trump's first term after serving on the National Security Council staff. He also had a short stint in the Office of the DNI. He came to the White House after working as a national security staffer on the Hill. Patel started his career as a public defender in Florida and later moved to the Justice Department. As FBI director, he is following the president's guidance to restructure the agency. Patel has also been appointed acting director of the Bureau of Alcohol, Tobacco, Firearms and Explosives.

- **Kevin Lunday | Acting Commandant of the Coast Guard**—Lunday is a career Coast Guard officer who rose to the rank of vice commandant before assuming the lead role in an acting capacity. He does not have a political background. As acting commandant, he will work on fortifying American security in the Western hemisphere and closer to its borders.

- **Martin Makary | Commissioner of the Food and Drug Administration (FDA)**—Makary is a renowned surgeon at Johns Hopkins Hospital and a lead professor at its medical school. He has published on what he calls the "surgeon checklist." He has a media background as an author and commentator, and *The Resident,* a television series, is based on one of his books. As FDA director, he will be engaged in the chronic disease epidemic and moving away from an overmedicated stance.

- **Mehmet Oz (nominee) | Administrator of Centers for Medicare and Medicaid Services (CMS)**—Oz entered the political arena by running for Senate in Pennsylvania in 2022, losing the race to Democratic candidate John Fetterman. His career began as a heart surgeon, and he rose to prominence in New York City in that capacity. This led to a television show and a close working relationship with Oprah Winfrey for decades. Oz also has extensive business interests. As CMS administrator, he will be expected to cut down on fraud and waste in the $1.5 trillion body.

- **Michael W. Banks | Chief of the United States Border Patrol (USBP)**—Banks was a career border patrol officer, rising to deputy chief. He resigned over disagreements with the Biden administration's border policy in 2023 and began work as an advisor to Texas Governor Abbott. As USBP chief, he is cooperating closely with other partners in the government and neighboring countries to bring illegal crossings as close to zero as possible.

- **Paul Atkins (nominee) | Chair of the Securities and Exchange Commission (SEC)**—Atkins has served as an SEC commissioner and as a staff member for other SEC chairs. He began his career as a lawyer and went on to found a boutique advisory firm. Recently, he has become known for his advocacy for treating crypto as a security. As SEC chair, he will formalize the regulation of digital assets.

- **Scott Kupor (nominee) | Director of the Office of Personnel Management (OPM)**—Kupor most recently served as managing director of the venture capital firm Andreessen Horowitz, where he was also its earliest employee. He previously worked as a corporate executive.

As OPM director, he will work closely with DOGE to pare back the size of the federal workforce.

- **Sean Curran | Director of Secret Service**—Curran was famously captured in the photo of Trump shortly after the assassination attempt in the summer of 2024. He has been in charge of his detail for four years and has served in the Secret Service since 2001. As Secret Service director, he has a close relationship with the president and will refocus its protection mandate.

- **Troy Meink (nominee) | Secretary of Air Force**—Meink was a career Air Force officer who joined the National Reconnaissance Office and was eventually appointed principal deputy director. He has a background in space and satellite systems. As Air Force secretary, he is anticipated to expand space capabilities and try to modernize the agency.

This is not the complete list of personnel heading government bodies, but they represent the critical functions. That being said, there are vital foreign missions. High-profile ambassadors nominated include Mike Huckabee (ambassador to Israel) and David Perdue (ambassador to China). Within the Department of Justice, two nominated U.S. attorneys are worth noting: Jay Clayton (Southern District of New York) and Edward Martin (Washington, DC).

Some positions remained unannounced or unchanged at the time of publication, notably the heads of the National Security Agency, the National Reconnaissance Office, and the Defense Intelligence Agency. In other cases, interim directors who may not be in their positions for an extended period have been appointed. This includes former Navy SEAL Cameron Hamilton as the interim administrator of the Federal Emergency Management Agency (FEMA). Also, an appointment does not mean that it will last. For example, Caleb Vitello survived as the acting director for ICE for just one month before being replaced.

Elected Officials

While the second Trump administration will revolve around the executive branch, other elected officials in Congress and the states are central to implementing the Trump 2.5 agenda.

Congress

The Senate is more critical than the House at the outset. Senate approval is required for most of the nominees for departments, agencies, and ambassadorial roles. Attention will then quickly move to judicial appointments.

Senate

There are 100 senators, and the president of the Senate is Vice President JD Vance, who votes in case of a tie. The Republicans have control over the Senate, with 53 senators and 47 for the Democrats (officially, Senators Angus King and Bernie Sanders are independent, but they caucus with the Democrats). There are several senators worth highlighting who are partners, partisans, or both for the White House.

- **Bill Hagerty (R-Tennessee)**—Senator Hagerty is an ally of Trump and served as the ambassador to Japan during his first term. After a business career, he ran for Senate in 2020. Based on his track record, Hagerty will presumably be engaged on technology legislation.
- **Chuck Grassley (R-Iowa)**—Senator Grassley is the president of the Senate in the vice president's absence and chairs the Judiciary Committee. He was elected to the Senate in 1980 after serving in the House of Representatives. Grassley is pivotal in moving judicial appointments from the White House forward.
- **Cynthia Lummis (R-Wyoming)**—Senator Lummis is the chair of the Senate Banking Subcommittee on Digital Assets. She began her political career as a representative,

initially at the state and then at the federal level, and she won her Senate seat in 2020. Lummis has been a staunch partisan for the president and is at the forefront of crypto policy.

- **John Thune (R-South Dakota)**—Senator Thune is the majority leader in the Senate and was considered close to Trump antagonist Senator Mitch McConnell. After three terms in the House, he contested and won a seat in the Senate in 2004. Thune is seen as a consensus builder in the Republican Party. While not considered part of the new MAGA wing, he has been a close partner of the president in advancing nominees at a record pace.
- **Joni Ernst (R-Iowa)**—Senator Ernst is the fourth-ranking Republican in the Senate and chair of the DOGE Caucus. She joined the Iowa State Senate and was elected to the U.S. Senate in 2014. Ernst has become close to Elon Musk and has been vocal about cutting what she terms government waste.
- **Josh Hawley (R-Missouri)**—Senator Hawley was an early promoter of President Trump's message of economic populism in the Senate. After serving as Missouri's attorney general, he won a Senate seat in 2018. He began his career in private legal practice before becoming a professor. Hawley will look to be the bipartisan driver of legislation on the White House's economic and labor policies.
- **Marsha Blackburn (R-Tennessee)**—Senator Blackburn was an early backer of Trump and served as a vice-chair of his transition team in 2016. She joined the Senate in 2021 after serving in the House for nearly two decades following a business career. Blackburn is an effective communications surrogate for the White House agenda on cable television.

- **Mike Lee (R-Utah)**—Senator Lee is the chair of the Energy Committee and the dean of Utah's congressional delegation. He alternated between private practice as a lawyer and government roles before winning a Senate seat in 2010. Lee has one of the most active accounts from the Senate on X, routinely joining Spaces to mobilize for the MAGA agenda.

- **Rand Paul (R-Kentucky)**—Senator Paul is the chair of the Homeland Security Committee and the son of the popular Republican politician, Ron Paul. He practiced medicine for almost two decades and then won a Senate seat in 2010. He avoided endorsing President Trump's re-election and opposed aspects of his agenda, particularly regarding tariffs, Israel, and labor. Paul is a proponent of RFK Jr. as he drives forward his version of health reform.

- **Rick Scott (R-Florida)**—Senator Scott unsuccessfully pursued the position of Senate majority leader as a more MAGA-oriented candidate, losing the vote to his colleague Senator Thune. After a lucrative career building health-related businesses, he served as Florida governor for two terms in the 2010s and won a Senate seat in 2018. Due in part to his links to Florida, Scott has made inroads with the Trump White House.

- **Ron Johnson (R-Wisconsin)**—Senator Johnson is the chair of the Subcommittee on Investigations. He ran a plastics business for decades before becoming a senator after the 2010 election. He emerged as an enthusiastic champion of President Trump during his first term. Johnson will use his subcommittee's power to push back on parts of the government hindering the White House agenda.

- **Ted Cruz (R-Texas)**—Senator Cruz chairs the Commerce Committee, one of the largest committees in the Senate.

Early in his career, he was a lawyer in private practice before joining the Department of Justice during the George W. Bush administration. He then became the solicitor general of Texas before successfully running for the Senate in 2012. While a rival to Trump in 2016, Cruz has since emerged as one of his most steadfast allies and will aim to further transportation and space policies.

- **Tom Cotton (R-Arkansas)**—Senator Cotton is the Chair of the Senate Intelligence Committee and Senate Republican Conference. After his military service, during which he served in both Iraq and Afghanistan, he briefly worked for a consulting firm. He became a congressman before running successfully for the Senate in 2014. He is one of the foreign policy hawks of the Senate and is at times on the other side of Trump's agenda. That being said, he backed the nomination of Tulsi Gabbard for DNI. Cotton will help shape the overhaul of the intelligence apparatus.
- **Tommy Tuberville (R-Alabama)**—Senator Tuberville is one of the stalwarts for President Trump and his agenda in the Senate. The championship-winning college football coach successfully ran for senate in 2020 without any political background. He is effectively a benchmark for Trump's loyalty in the Senate.

John Barrasso (R-Wyoming), Lindsey Graham (R-South Carolina), John Kennedy (R-Louisiana), and Tim Scott (R-South Carolina) are other senators who could be listed here. They have each been vocal advocates of the president in recent years. Given their senior positions, they may partner to forward parts of the White House agenda. In addition, Roger Wicker (R-Mississippi), the chair of the Committee on Armed Services, will be engaged when required on defense matters.

Jim Banks (R-Indiana), Katie Britt (R-Alabama), Ted Budd (R-North Carolina), Bernie Moreno (R-Ohio), Jim Justice

(R-West Virginia), Markwayne Mullin (R-Oklahoma), Eric Schmitt (R-Missouri), and Tim Sheehy (R-Montana) are part of a more recent group of junior senators who are further removed from the McConnell era and associate themselves closely with President Trump. They may emerge to play roles in advancing the Trump 2.5 agenda. Over the next 12 to 18 months, the most essential Republican senators will become clear, as this is an evolving landscape.

There are senators who, over the years, have served to obstruct Trump, politically or administratively, on different issues. They could undermine the Republican majority in the Senate. This group includes Susan Collins (R-Maine), Mitch McConnell (R-Kentucky), Todd Young (R-Indiana), Bill Cassidy (R-Louisiana), John Cornyn (R-Texas), and Lisa Murkowski (R-Alaska).

Democratic senators who might be interlocutors for the Trump 2.5 agenda have yet to emerge. However, Bernie Sanders (I-Vermont) and John Fetterman (D-Pennsylvania) have expressed openness to joining the new president to advance policies on reducing credit card interest rates, for example.

House

The House of Representatives has 435 members, and, as noted, the Republican majority is razor thin. With the presidential appointment of Mike Waltz (R-Florida) to the White House and the resignation of Matt Gaetz (R-Florida), the total number of Republican-held seats came down to 218. Two special elections held in Florida on April 1, 2025, restored the GOP majority to 220 seats; a special election in New York for Elise Stefanik's seat was avoided after her nomination was withdrawn. The Speaker of the House must navigate all legislative moments carefully. This section highlights a handful of members in the House who are more visible and are worth following to understand trend lines. Given that there are over 200 Republicans in the chamber, this is by no means an exhaustive list and should only be used for indicative purposes.

- **Abe Hamadeh (R-Arizona)**—Representative Hamadeh is a freshman congressman who defeated Peter Thiel's acolyte, Blake Masters, in a contested race in 2024. Prior to entering politics, he was a county prosecutor and served in the U.S. Army Reserve. Hamadeh is one of the more vigorous MAGA champions and is already active on the administration's agenda on the Hill. His press secretary, Alexis Wilkins, is also the girlfriend of FBI Director Kash Patel.

- **Andy Biggs (R-Arizona)**—Representative Biggs won election to the House in 2016 and is the chair of the Freedom Caucus. He co-led an alternative congressional investigation into the attempted assassination of President Trump. Earlier in his career, he was a prosecutor, but after winning a $10 million publisher's sweepstakes, and with financial independence, he ran for the state house. Biggs may run for Arizona governor and is an enthusiastic partner for the Trump agenda.

- **Anna Paulina Luna (R-Florida)**—Representative Luna was elected in 2022. She emerged through the ranks of Turning Point USA and was a social media influencer for the MAGA movement before running. Prior to her political turn, she was a model, appearing in *Maxim*, and served in the Air Force. Luna has been implacable in backing the president and allies and is a reliable vote for the MAGA movement.

- **Byron Donalds (R- Florida)**—Representative Donalds ran successfully for Congress in 2020. He was a surrogate for President Trump during the 2024 presidential election cycle and was the most visible African American on the campaign trail. Before Congress, he served in the Florida House after a career as a financial analyst. Donalds has stated he will run for Florida governor and will continue to be a reliable backer of the president.

- **James Comer (R-Kentucky)**—Representative Comer won his seat in 2016 and is chair of the Oversight Committee. He has been a staunch defender of the president and was active in probing for further details behind the assassination attempts targeting Trump. After a career as a farmer, he had political roles in Kentucky, where he may yet run for governor. Comer is working closely with the White House to promote government efficiency.

- **Jim Jordan (R-Ohio)**—Representative Jordan has been in Congress since winning his seat in 2006 and chairs the Judiciary Committee. He has played a noticeable role in addressing what he sees as the weaponization of government. Before joining the U.S. House, he was a wrestling coach, state representative, and state senator. Jordan is one of the original MAGA supporters on the Hill. However, the degree to which he will align with the current Republican House leadership, which he had contested, is uncertain.

- **Lauren Boebert (R-Colorado)**—Representative Boebert rose out of relative obscurity to win a seat in Congress in 2020. Since then, she has been in the spotlight as a firebrand partisan for the MAGA agenda. Prior to her political career, she owned and operated a restaurant. During Trump's second term, she is anticipated to be an active surrogate when needed.

- **Marjorie Taylor Greene (R-Georgia)**—Representative Greene won a seat in the House in 2020 and quickly became 'ultra-MAGA.' She found her political moorings by backing Rep. Kevin McCarthy in his bid for the Speaker position in 2023, actively back-channeling with Trump. In the current congressional term, she chairs the newly created DOGE subcommittee. Before working on the hill, she owned and operated a CrossFit gym. Greene will hold investigative hearings to complement the activities of DOGE.

- **Mike Johnson (R-Louisiana)**—Speaker Johnson joined Congress after succeeding in the 2016 election. He won the Speaker role as a surprising choice after the ouster of Kevin McCarthy. While facing skepticism from the MAGA base, he has a solid relationship with the White House. Prior to joining the U.S. House, he served briefly in the Louisiana House after a legal and non-profit career. Johnson's test will be managing a legislative and budget process to match the White House's speed and ambition.

- **Nancy Mace (R-South Carolina)**—Representative Mace ran successfully for Congress in 2020. While she was a field director for the first Trump presidential campaign in 2016, she diverged from the president over the January 6 attacks. Before her political career, she was a public relations consultant and served in the military after having started her work life at the Waffle House. Mace's stance on transgender policy has elevated her profile, but it is not certain how close she will be to the White House during Trump's second term.

- **Paul Gosar (R-Arizona)**—Representative Gosar was elected to the House in 2010 and was endorsed by Trump for re-election after facing censure from his peers. Before joining Congress, he was a dentist. He is one of the reliable stalwarts on every aspect of the MAGA agenda and may lead probes into big tech and voter transparency.

- **Steve Scalise (R-Louisiana)**—Representative Scalise was elected to Congress in 2008 and is the House majority leader. In June 2017, Scalise was shot and seriously injured during a domestic terrorist attack on the annual Congressional Baseball Game. Initially working as a software engineer, he joined the Louisiana House at a young age before eventually pursuing federal politics. Scalise is a point person on the budgetary cuts the administration is trying to undertake.

Eli Crane (R-Arizona), Mary Miller (R-Illinois), Cory Mills (R-Florida), and other representatives could have been listed here. In effect, any one representative has a limited role. It will be more interesting to see if a group emerges to form a new caucus that prompts new group dynamics to facilitate the Trump 2.5 agenda.

Chip Roy (R-Texas), Tom Emmer (R-Minnesota), and Thomas Massie (R-Kentucky) are part of a handful of Republican members of Congress who have occasionally opposed part of Trump's agenda over the years. Massie is interesting because while he and Trump have clashed publicly, he resonates well with much of the online MAGA community.

Dan Newhouse (R-Washington) and David Valadao (R-California) are the only Republican representatives who voted to impeach Donald Trump who remain in the House. They need to be managed adroitly by Speaker Johnson to keep them onside.

At times, Democratic representatives will choose to cross the aisle and vote affirmatively on Republican proposals, particularly those related to immigration and the border. Ro Khanna (D-California), who has a pro-technology lens, may get behind aspects of the Trump 2.5 agenda. As in the first term, partisan fervor in the House will make bipartisanship challenging, although it can occur as it did in the case of the First Step Act in 2018.

States

Governors are pivotal to the adoption of the Trump 2.5 agenda. There are a total of 27 Republican governors. Republican-led states will provide staying power beyond the administration's four years for the MAGA movement.

Additionally, states will assume added responsibilities as the Trump White House devolves federal powers in education, emergency management, and other files. Republican governors are also considering mimicking moves made at the federal level, establishing their own departments of government efficiency. A few Republican governors actively facilitating the Trump 2.5 agenda are worth highlighting.

- **Bill Lee (R-Tennessee)**—Governor Lee assumed office in 2019 and had a brief dust-up with President Trump in 2024 as they backed rival candidates in a state primary. Prior to politics, he led his family's construction business. Lee will replicate federal moves on school vouchers, immigration, and government efficiency at the state level.

- **Greg Abbott (R-Texas)**—Governor Abbott assumed office in 2015 in a state with a $2.5 trillion economy today. He has become increasingly close to President Trump on immigration. In addition, Elon Musk and his companies have a growing presence in Texas. Abbott will try to shape Texas as a fulcrum for federal policies on a state level.

- **Jeff Landry (R-Louisiana)**—Governor Landry assumed office in 2024 after obtaining Trump's endorsement in the Republican primary. He is seen as a staunch MAGA supporter and hosted President Trump during Super Bowl LIX. Before the governorship, he was attorney general and, prior to that, a congressman. He started his career as a lawyer but soon entered politics. Landry is a champion of the president's offshore energy priorities.

- **Kevin Stitt (R-Oklahoma)**—Governor Stitt is the first Native American governor in the country, hailing from the Cherokee Nation. He assumed office in 2019, and Trump campaigned for him in the election. Before political office, he built and led a residential mortgage company. Stitt is aligning his state with the federal government's tax and spending policies and has replicated the DOGE agency at the state level.

- **Kim Reynolds (R-Iowa)**—Governor Reynolds assumed office in 2017 and fell out of favor with Trump when she endorsed Ron DeSantis for the 2024 presidential election. Following Trump's victory in November, she made repeated visits to Mar-a-Lago to bridge the divide. She served as a county official before becoming a state senator and then lieutenant governor. Reynolds is another state executive backing the government's efficiency plans.

- **Ron DeSantis (R-Florida)**—Governor DeSantis assumed office in 2019 and was President Trump's principal opponent during the Republican primary in his bid for re-election. While they have since developed a working relationship, they are not considered close. He began his career as a legal officer in the Navy and ran for Congress in 2012. DeSantis is a partner of the administration on the priority of immigration and the devolution of federal powers to states.

- **Sarah Huckabee Sanders (R-Arkansas)**—Governor Huckabee Sanders assumed office in 2023 after serving as press secretary in the White House during the first Trump term. She is the daughter of former governor Mike Huckabee and has been active in Republican politics for years across several campaigns. Huckabee Sanders is on the 2024 executive committee of the Republican Governors Association and will play a decisive role as a state-level leader, mobilizing other governors to support the president's agenda.

Others who could be listed here include Kelly Ayotte (R-New Hampshire), Brad Little (R-Idaho), Jim Pillen (R-Nebraska), and Glenn Youngkin (R-Virginia). Other nationally known officials below the governor level who are vocal MAGA advocates include Ken Paxton and Andrew Bailey, the attorneys general of Texas and Missouri, respectively.

The Republican Governors Association's leadership team, which includes Chair Brian Kemp (R-Georgia), Vice Chair Greg Gianforte (R-Montana), and Policy Chair Henry McMaster (R-SC), does not include vocal allies of the president. This will probably change over the next four years.

While most Democratic governors disapprove of the Trump 2.5 agenda, there are opportunities for compromise. On infrastructure, given California's size, it is conceivable that Trump will attempt collaboration with that state's governor, Gavin Newsom. Similarly, Jared Polis (D-Colorado) has been close to Robert F. Kennedy Jr. and may facilitate policies that reform the food supply in the country.

Kathy Hochul (D-New York) and JB Pritzker (D-Illinois) represent two of the country's four largest economies and firmly oppose the president and his agenda. They may face upcoming electoral challenges. Meanwhile, the White House will try to use federal funding restrictions to shift state opposition to policies.

Media Platforms

Today, the media includes traditional news media, disruptive digital publications, and individuals simply streaming. President Trump considers engagement with all a plus in that it brings attention, even with networks that have often slanted coverage against him, although that has not stopped him from suing those same networks.

Television

White House officials regularly appear on television, reflecting the president's ubiquity. However, some stations may be favored.

- **CNBC**—The network is seen as the station of record for pushing economic messages. Administration officials often join the show *Squawk Box*. Its co-host, Joe Kernan, was a vocal defender of the president's campaign in 2024.

- **Fox News**—The mainstay of conservative opinion has had a mixed editorial relationship with Trump. Various talk show hosts, notably Jeanine Pirro, Greg Gutfeld, Laura Ingraham, the co-hosts of *Fox & Friends*, Harris Faulkner, Maria Bartiromo, and Sean Hannity, have close relationships with the president.

- **Newsmax**—The right-wing television channel launched in 2014, building on its widely read digital publication. It is a go-to station for friendly interviews with administration officials. Rob Schmitt, Chris Salcedo, and Greg Kelly are hosts who have interviewed Trump in the past year.

- **One American News (OAN)**—OAN launched a decade ago but today has a limited cable footprint, relying on digital views. It is firmly within the MAGA camp and recently recruited former Congressman Matt Gaetz as a host. Their White House correspondent, Daniel Baldwin, has solid access, and their primetime host, Dan Ball, had a one-on-one interview with Trump following the election.

As demonstrated early in the administration, the major networks—ABC, CBS, and NBC—are being engaged, particularly the Sunday talk shows. While most shows on MSNBC have had a partisan bias for the Democrats, akin to Fox News for the GOP, *Morning Joe* will presumably chase an interview with Trump at some point. Other rising stations, like NewsNation, may also be engaged as an alternative messaging outlet. Finally, CNN, which President Trump regularly calls fake news, has one of the most visible pro-Trump analysts on cable news, Scott Jennings. Despite criticizing the administration, its White House correspondent, Kaitlin Collins, has solid access, although that may change.

Print

There are few print—or digital-cum-print—publications that the Trump administration would consider onside and that also have a wide reach.

- **Breitbart**—The conservative publication became a go-to platform for Republicans involved in the Tea Party movement in the 2010s. After its founder and namesake died in 2012, it was led by Stephen Bannon for the years leading up to Trump's rise. There is much more competition today, and it is not central to the Republican populist conversation. Its editor-in-chief is Alex Marlowe, and the Washington bureau chief is Matt Boyle; he interviewed the president in late 2024.

- **Los Angeles Times**—A top-five newspaper in the United States, it underwent an editorial shift in the lead-up to the 2024 election under its owner, Patrick Soon-Shiong. Considered the wealthiest person in Los Angeles, Soon-Shiong pulled his paper's editorial board back from endorsing Kamala Harris and has tried to adjust coverage after the election. CNN commentator Scott Jennings has been added in a lead role.

- **New York Post**—One of the oldest newspapers in the country, the *New York Post* is considered a tabloid. While the paper has sometimes outright mocked Trump on its covers, it has also echoed select themes of the president and endorsed him in the 2024 election. The *Post* also broke the Hunter Biden laptop story in 2020.

- **The Free Press**—The FP, as it is known, was founded by former *New York Times* staffer Bari Weiss as part of the anti-cancel culture movement. It has since become associated with a somewhat tapered-down form of

Trumpism that holds an editorial line of being anti-woke and pro-Israel. The platform and its investors are closely associated with the new techno-political wing buttressing the administration.

The Trump White House sees *The New York Times*, *The Washington Post*, and, at times, *The Wall Street Journal* as opposition press. Given the president's background in New York, they are still engaged due to his familiarity with them. His team prepares a regular printout of articles from these and other newspapers for him. One publication that may see a shift is *Time* magazine, owned by Salesforce CEO Marc Benioff. President Trump gave the magazine an extended interview after being named its "Person of the Year" in December 2024.

Other digital conservative platforms—e.g., *The Federalist*, *Free Beacon*, and *Gateway Pundit*—have also risen in prominence during the last decade. Finally, it is difficult to evaluate other publications with substantial reach that rely on backlinks and news aggregation, notably *USA Today* and the *Daily Mail*.

Allies

While the executive and legislative branches of the government are pivotal for the Trump agenda, as are traditional media platforms, the constellation of allies on the outside is as relevant. This includes supporters, sponsors, and online voices. There is a continuum, especially since the appointment of Elon Musk, between outside allies and the administration. A midnight Space on X in early February, for example, brought together a mix of senators, journalists, influencers, and business tycoons alongside Musk to discuss DOGE just as it was taking shape.

Supporters

The emergence of a third rail in the online discourse from Silicon Valley proved to be a wildcard in the election cycle. They form a backbone of supporters who possess institutional heft and complement existing MAGA supporters like Stephen Bannon and Charlie Kirk, also listed below. During inauguration week, many of these supporters were the hosts and co-hosts of a number of parties. This group, who mostly straddle techno-optimism or economic populism, all have independent platforms and resources. While today they are in alignment, they may not be tomorrow.

- **Balaji Srinivasan**—The entrepreneur and former crypto executive promotes a decentralized future. While most of the network of technologists who pushed for political change are based in the U.S., he moved to Singapore during the COVID-19 pandemic and is less engaged in the current administration as it takes shape.

- **Bill Ackman**—The hedge fund founder was early in criticizing DEI and backing Trump within the business community. While not from the technology space, he is engaged in the same networks. He is vocal about Israel and antisemitism.

- **Calley Means**—The co-author with his sister Casey Means of the number one bestseller *Good Energy: The Surprising Connection between Metabolism and Limitless Health* is credited with bringing Trump and Robert F. Kennedy Jr. together in 2024. Means is a former policy consultant who is instrumental to the MAHA movement.

- **Chamath Palihapitiya**—The venture capitalist co-host of the *All-in* podcast, with David Sacks, actively mobilized Silicon Valley for Trump. He was an early employee at Facebook and founded Social Capital. With Sacks in government, Palihapitiya will echo messages on the outside.

- **Charlie Kirk**—The founder of Turning Point USA is one of the fulcrums of the entire MAGA movement, even though he is only in his early 30s. He and the TPUSA organization worked closely with Lara Trump and the RNC in the 2024 presidential election to register voters and ensure turnout. The party he co-hosted at the inauguration was one of the most well-attended.

- **Chris Pavlovski**—The Canadian founder of the streaming platform Rumble has emerged as a close partner of the new administration. With investors Thiel, Ramaswamy, and JD Vance in 2021, the platform began to have a period of sustained growth. In February, the White House set up an official channel on Rumble.

- **Dana White**—The founder and CEO of UFC introduced Trump at the Republican National Convention shortly after the first assassination attempt. As a longtime friend, he emerged as an intersection point for Trump and the young male vote. He helped arrange Trump's appearance on *The Joe Rogan Experience*.

- **Joe Lonsdale**—The venture capitalist is a co-founder of Palantir. He is close to Peter Thiel, with links from his early days at PayPal and connections through Stanford. He also has a good relationship with Elon Musk.

- **Larry Ellison**—The founder of Oracle and deca-billionaire is a close friend of Elon Musk and has invested in his ventures. Ellison showed up early to the White House during the second term to attend the Stargate AI announcement.

- **Marc Benioff**—The Salesforce founder and owner of *Time* was an advocate of policies aligned with the Democratic Party. During the 2024 presidential campaign, he tweeted his support for Trump and derided Harris for her lack of media availability. His shift, along with that of other Fortune 500 CEOs, is creating a new business base for the MAGA-led GOP.

- **Marc Andreessen**—The co-founder of Netscape and leading venture capitalist in Silicon Valley is a self-declared 'accelerationist.' Before and after the election, he created ideological coherence among technologists favoring the Trump 2.5 era. As a sizable investor in AI and crypto, his voice matters as much as anyone else's in the administration's policies.

- **Mike Solana**—The founder of the digital publication *Pirate Wires* is another acolyte of Peter Thiel's and works at his venture capital fund. His publication is arguably the most well-read platform covering the undercurrents of the techno-political world.

- **Naval Ravikant**—The co-founder of AngelList has evolved in recent years into a techno-guru, with multiple books to that effect. His entry into the discourse during the election cycle in 2024 by backing Trump was a shock, as he had almost always remained apolitical. As one of the most respected individuals in the technology community, he has influenced followers to take a more favorable view of Trump.

- **Nicole Shanahan**—The lawyer and health advocate was married to Google founder Sergey Brin. That divorce left her with sizable wealth, and when she found common cause with RFK Jr., she became a financial backer of his campaign for president in 2024 and eventually his vice presidential pick. After RFK Jr. endorsed Trump for the presidency, Shanahan helped formalize the MAHA movement. Since the election, she has continued to use her platform and finances to ensure support for the MAHA agenda and RFK Jr.'s nomination process. She may join the administration in some capacity.

- **Omeed Malik**—The venture capitalist is a backer of Tucker Carlson's new media venture through his firm 1789 Capital. Following the election, Donald Trump Jr. also joined 1789. Malik contributed to RFK Jr.'s campaign and built a close relationship with Tulsi Gabbard. He is a financial node for the new MAGA media ecosystem.

- **Peter Thiel**—One of his era's foremost investors and technologists, Thiel has a mixed relationship with both Elon Musk and Donald Trump. However, he spoke at the Republican National Convention in 2016. He had a guiding role in JD Vance's career, and now many of his protégés dot the administration at both senior and junior levels.

- **Shaun Maguire**—The Sequoia Capital partner broke the proverbial ice in the Bay Area with an early announcement in favor of Trump in the spring of 2024. Partly motivated by policy vis-à-vis Israel, he helped mobilize an online conversation that shifted the business and technology community to Trump's side. This role has continued post-election.

- **Stephen Bannon**—The modern godfather of the populist movement within the Republican Party hosts the political podcast *War Room*. While he played a role in the 2016 campaign and early days of Trump's first term, he has been less involved formally since. Just a week before the election, Bannon was released from prison, where he served a sentence for contempt of court in a political inquiry. Since the election, he has jousted with Elon Musk and has tried to reinforce an economic populist message.

- **Tucker Carlson**—The ubiquitous media personality is scaling the Tucker Carlson Network, backed by Omeed Malik. Once the lead host on Fox News and cable news, Carlson bucked the traditional conservative crowd to become an informal advisor to Trump. He has become a lightning rod for criticism from establishment Republicans.

- **Vivek Ramaswamy**—As an entrepreneur, he was a dark horse candidate in the 2024 Republican Primary. His early endorsement of Trump and engaging presence on the campaign trail brought him into the limelight. In February 2025, he returned to Ohio to enter the gubernatorial race.

Sponsors

In addition to the roster of supporters, a group of donors has played an outsized role behind the scenes. They have been very active in donating considerable sums (for this election cycle).

- **Ken Griffin**—The founder of the investment firm Citadel is a crucial Republican Party backer. He preliminarily funded DeSantis's presidential bid but then withdrew support. While he donated around $100 million to Republican candidates, his relationship with Trump and the MAGA movement is decidedly mixed. He criticized the president's economic policies after his re-election.

- **Miriam Adelson**—The widow of casino magnate Sheldon Adelson continues his legacy as a Republican donor. After a tense back-and-forth in the final weeks of the election cycle, she delivered $100 million to the Trump campaign. Her one overriding concern is standing with Israel.

- **Stephen Schwarzman**—The co-founder of private equity firm Blackstone was an early donor in the New York business community, publicly backing Trump in 2024. In addition to making significant political donations, he hosted major fundraisers for the president with the business community.

- **Timothy Mellon**—The heir to the Mellon fortune was arguably the biggest donor of the 2024 election cycle, backing RFK Jr. initially. It is estimated that he later donated upwards of $125 million to Trump-associated PACs. He stays out of the limelight.

There are other prominent donors within Republican circles. Paul Singer and the family of Robert Mercer were more engaged in the past but are seen as less enthusiastic partisans moving forward for the MAGA movement. However, they are still very active in contributing funds to GOP candidates. Two other couples are less prominent but worth mentioning as their contributions to Trump's re-election exceeded $50 million each: the Wisconsin-based Richard and Elizabeth Uihlein, and Jeffrey and Janine Yass, based in Pennsylvania, who are investors in ByteDance, the Chinese parent of TikTok. Elon Musk is not listed here; according to reports, he may have contributed upwards of $250 million in the recent election cycle.

America Online

The discussion of politics has shifted to the online universe. Given its numbers and diversity, mapping it is nearly impossible. Yet, there are figures who, in effect, move the needle and translate online sentiment into offline results.

They are listed across four categories: MAGA, converts, streamers, and 'out there.' Most individuals are on Truth Social, X, YouTube, Rumble, Kick, or other streaming platforms. While Instagram and TikTok provide amplification, these platforms are less pivotal for driving the debate in the MAGA movement.

MAGA

Unlike in 2015, when the MAGA movement was affiliated in the public eye with an 'alt-right' that existed on the fringes, today, it is in the mainstream. There are also MAGA-adjacent voices, such as Glenn Beck and Ben Shapiro, who are considered traditional conservatives but are in the broad tent, and more neutral voices, like John Solomon and Jonathan Turley.

- **Alex Bruesewitz**—The social media advisor manages branded accounts online in an outside role for a Trump PAC. During the 2024 campaign, he prepared and executed the podcast strategy, which was instrumental in informing the Gen Z vote.
- **Alex Lorusso**—The conservative media strategist became close to Elon Musk as one of his conduits in the MAGA movement. He is well connected with Charlie Kirk and Benny Johnson.
- **Amanda Milius**—The daughter of a famed Hollywood director, she has been in the inner MAGA circle since the beginning of the first Trump presidency. She directed a movie about the Russia investigation, *The Plot Against the President*.
- **amuse**—This anonymous online account promotes an anti-establishment discourse that occasionally adopts a racialized tone. Raw Egg Nationalist is a similar account that advances a nativist identity. @amuse is representative of this group of heavily amplified accounts and is often retweeted by Musk.
- **Andy Ngo**—An editor at the digital publication *The Post Millennial*, he rose to prominence in his coverage of Antifa protests during the first Trump term. He has been part of the anti-woke movement but is not considered ideologically aligned with MAGA.
- **Ashley St. Clair**—The online personality was an early figure in a connected group of conservative women influencers on Twitter. She has worked at the *Babylon Bee* and amplified Vivek Ramaswamy and Elon Musk during the campaign. In February, she stated that she and Musk had a child together.

- **Ben Shapiro**—The co-founder with Jeremy Boreing of the conservative media conglomerate *The Daily Wire* has a top political podcast. However, two of his former staff members, Candace Owens and Brett Cooper, have since overtaken him in the rankings. Still, he remains one of the most in-demand conservative speakers on college campuses. He continues to clash with Tucker Carlson on foreign policy.

- **Benny Johnson**—One of the most followed conservative voices online, he has a podcast called *The Benny Show*. He was embroiled in a Russian influence operation alongside fellow YouTuber Tim Pool. He brings vast amplification to conservative guests.

- **Chaya Raichik**—The influencer runs the once anonymous account Libs of TikTok, which *The Washington Post* doxxed. The account, which has over 3 million followers on X, exposes what it conveys as woke ideology in schools and was itself accused of doxxing individuals. She continues to have direct access to the president's communications team.

- **CJ Pearson**—The online personality also serves as co-chair of the RNC's Youth Advisory Council. He actively mobilized the young conservative vote for Trump in the 2024 election. He brought together multiple influencers for inauguration festivities, which were featured on the cover of *New York Magazine*.

- **Christopher Rufo**—As a senior fellow at the Manhattan Institute, he has spearheaded the charge against critical race theory and the DEI movement. He has been closer to Ron DeSantis and some Never Trump individuals, although Trump administration officials have brought him in to advise on aspects of government reform.

- **Dan Bongino**—The former Secret Service agent turned talk show host was fired from Fox News around the same time as Tucker Carlson. An early convert to the YouTube alternative *Rumble*, he became a shareholder before its IPO. The White House has named him deputy director of the Federal Bureau of Investigation.

- **Dave Rubin**—The conservative influencer has one of YouTube's top political accounts. He was victim to the same Russian operation that ensnared Benny Johnson and Tim Pool. After endorsing Ron DeSantis in the primary, Rubin has been somewhat on the periphery of the Trump ecosystem but remains very connected in Republican circles.

- **FischerKing**—This anonymous account posts philosophical and social commentary, which is amplified heavily within conservative circles. It forms part of a smaller ideological MAGA circle that drives discussion online.

- **Glenn Beck**—The media personality has been on the scene since the mid-2000s. He rose to prominence on Fox News and left to start his own streaming platform, The Blaze (now Blaze Media). Subsequently, the platform became insolvent but was merged with other conservative platforms in 2018. While he has a sizable audience, he is not core to the MAGA movement.

- **Jack Posobiec**—One of the original MAGA supporters is one of the most followed conservatives online. He worked as a U.S. Naval Intelligence officer and is fluent in Mandarin. He is an editor of the digital platform Human Events and often drives the online MAGA conversation. Posobiec is close to Stephen Bannon.

- **James O'Keefe**—The founder of the now-defunct Project Veritas pioneered the shock journalism of secret filming in the digital age. While his stories continue to resonate, contributing to the dismissal of government employees since the election, he has lost his footing in the last couple of years as the MAGA movement has become more established.

- **John Solomon**—A consummate newsman who has worked at the *AP, Washington Post, Washington Examiner,* and *Fox News*, he launched Justthenews.com in 2020 and writes about the media's coverage of the political arena. With his vast networks and presence in prominent outlets, Solomon brings some of Trump's narratives into the mainstream press.

- **Johnny Maga**—The representative anonymous MAGA account often amplifies short clips of Trump rallies or statements. Trump has re-shared posts from the account on Truth Social.

- **Jonathan Keeperman**—The former university lecturer is best known online as 'L0m3z' and founded the publishing platform Passage Press. The platform has profiled Steve Sailer and Curtis Yarvin, who has ties to Peter Thiel. Keeperman hosted the MAGA-centric inaugural event, the Coronation Ball, which was covered in *GQ*. He is a social glue for the online right.

- **Jonathan Turley**—The legal scholar provides a counter-narrative on mainstream media positions regarding lawfare against Trump. His dispassionate analysis offered conservative media platforms a voice to push back on the investigations against Trump in 2024. Since the election, he has returned to the airwaves to offer analysis of the administration's legal positions. He would not call himself a partisan or MAGA.

- **Julie Kelly**—The political commentator emerged as a voice on the right covering the cases of January 6 protestors. Her continued coverage created a steady pressure that led to the pardons eventually signed by President Trump, with whom she has an intermittent dialogue.

People and Positions 143

- **Matt Walsh**—A journalist at *The Daily Wire*, he highlights woke/anti-woke matters and has released viral documentaries about those themes. He has been influential in bringing opposition to gender ideology to a wider audience. While active in the public discourse, Walsh is less pivotal to public policy than Chris Rufo.

- **Michael Knowles**—The popular YouTuber affiliated with *The Daily Wire* is known for his culture warrior perspective. He has been a vocal advocate for Trump for nearly a decade. It will be interesting to see how Knowles and other culture warriors dovetail with figures from the new right, like Keeperman.

- **Mike Benz**—The self-proclaimed deep state whisperer is a former State Department official at the forefront of online discussion about auditing the U.S. government to prevent disinformation. Since the establishment of DOGE, his interviews and videos have become blueprints for some administration staff.

- **Mike Cernovich**—One of the original members of the MAGA movement, side-by-side with Posobiec, has continued to be a driver of the online conversation. He was a frequent Trump critic from the right in the second half of the first term and initially favored Ron DeSantis in the primary. Cernovich provides continued ideological mooring for MAGA at an intrinsic level and is connected with everyone from Musk to Donald Trump Jr.

- **Mike Flynn**—The former DIA director during Obama's presidency famously resigned as national security advisor in the early days of Trump's first term. He had been a harsh critic of American foreign policy in the Middle East. Since his resignation and subsequent prosecution, he has increasingly built a firebrand persona online. The documentary about his life, *Flynn*, released in 2024, has been popular in conservative circles.

- **Mollie Hemingway**—The editor-in-chief of the digital publication *The Federalist* is a regular guest on Fox News. Her 2021 book *Rigged*, which was informed by an interview with Trump, argued that the Democratic Party illegitimately captured the 2020 elections.

- **Natalie Winters**—The co-host of the Bannon-led podcast *War Room* caused a stir as the platform's White House correspondent due to some mainstream media criticism of her outfits. She represents a new cohort of young women who are conservative voices and social influencers. She has her own fashion brand.

- **Raheem Kassam**—The British political activist is very close to Stephen Bannon, dating back to their time at Breitbart. He also co-founded *War Room* and is today the editor-in-chief of the digital publication *The National Pulse*. He has had a working relationship with British conservative politician Nigel Farage. Kassam covered Trump closely during the election and has since traveled with the vice president to Europe.

- **Riley Gaines**—The student-athlete turned political activist became the most high-profile advocate on transgender athlete participation. She was present and called out by name by President Trump when he signed the executive order banning the participation of transgender males in female sports.

- **Robby Starbuck**—The music video director became a political activist in the late 2010s and had an unsuccessful bid for Congress. In 2024, he became a mobilizing force pushing corporate America to end DEI programs, targeting Fortune 500 companies. This effort gained steam after Trump's inauguration.

- **Ryan Fournier**—The online activist runs Students for Trump. While a rising voice, he was caught up in controversy in 2025 related to a TikTok-named meme coin.

- **Scott Adams**—The creator of the comic strip *Dilbert* has become a YouTuber with a substantial conservative following. He has focused on what he sees as dissembling language used by the Democratic Party.

- **Scott Pressler**—The conservative influencer worked on get-out-the-vote activities in Pennsylvania in 2024. He worked closely with Turning Point USA and Lara Trump at the RNC, and Musk partially funded his activities. Pressler is now expanding his organization to New Jersey.

- **Sean Davis**—The co-founder of *The Federalist* maintains a close relationship with Tucker Carlson from his days at the *Daily Caller*. He continues to be a behind-the-scenes connector within conservative media and narratives.

- **Tim Pool**—The multi-platform streamer was embroiled in the same Russian influence operation as Benny Johnson and Dave Rubin. His platform, *Timcast*, remains one of the most influential in MAGA circles, and he hosts a variety of guests and perspectives. He has less engagement with Republican politicians, mainly interviewing influencers.

- **ZeroHedge**—The finance-oriented news platform has a considerable following on social media. In 2020, its account was famously banned on Twitter after it linked the origins of the COVID-19 virus to Chinese researchers. The site's Bulgarian-born editor remains anonymous but guides its content. *ZeroHedge* has continued to influence the discussion of financial topics in conservative circles.

Due to space constraints, other individuals with reach who are influential in the MAGA movement have not been included here. In general, anonymous and aggregator accounts, which have far-reaching online followings, are mostly left out as they create more online noise and have fewer followers in political circles.

Converts

In recent years, a few figures from the political left (or center) have become tepid to vocal proponents of Donald Trump. An anti-war stance has been a driver, while others are active in the MAHA movement.

- **Alex Berenson**—The former *New York Times* reporter was arguably the leading critic of the government's policies responding to the COVID-19 pandemic. He has a well-read Substack. Berenson has alternated between lukewarm support for Trump and disapproval before and after his re-election.
- **Aaron Maté**—The Canadian journalist has emerged as a harsh critic of U.S. foreign policy, writing on Ukraine and Israel in recent years. He writes for the digital platform *The Grayzone*, founded by similarly minded Max Blumenthal. While Maté would not be described as a Trump partisan, he has been enthusiastic about Trump's threat to the U.S. security consensus.
- **Dave Smith**—A stand-up comedian and podcaster, Smith is also a libertarian political campaigner who has been outspoken about the conflict in Gaza. He eventually endorsed Trump, partly because of his commitment to commuting Ross Ulbricht's sentence.
- **Eric Weinstein**—The academic and investor became a critic of the media narrative surrounding the pandemic and continues to speak out against misinformation. He has worked for Peter Thiel. After the election, he has had robust online debates with MAGA personalities.
- **Glenn Greenwald**—The founder of *The Intercept* and national security journalist has a platform on Rumble. He made a hard pivot against what he sees as the liberal intersection with the security state to make common cause with the MAGA agenda. He remains skeptical of the current administration's stance on Israel.

- **Jessica Reed Kraus**—The Instagram superstar has a highly-ranked newsletter on Substack. While initially a Hillary Clinton voter, she became a MAHA champion in the 2024 election cycle and was pivotal in mobilizing the 'mom' vote for Trump. Similar to other RFK Jr. enthusiasts, her advocacy has continued post-election.

- **Jimmy Dore**—The stand-up comedian once was a vocal champion of Bernie Sanders but has since become a harsh critic of him and the Democratic Party. He now has a high number of YouTube followers and often intersects with Greenwald and other people formerly associated with the left. He disapproves of Trump's policies toward Israel but praises his dismantling of the bureaucracy.

- **Matt Taibbi**—The writer and cultural commentator became increasingly disparaging of the media in the late 2010s in response to the Russia investigation against Trump. He has a top-ranked Substack. Before clashing with Elon Musk, he was an interlocutor for the reporting of the Twitter Files. He remains a critic of the anti-disinformation complex and co-hosts the podcast *America This Week* with novelist Walter Kirn.

- **Russell Brand**—The high-profile English entertainer became associated with the American right in 2024. He appeared on stage with Tucker Carlson and is a fan of RFK Jr. and the MAHA movement. He commands a vast online following and also hosts a podcast. He reportedly is under criminal investigation in the United Kingdom regarding his personal conduct.

This may be a growing segment of those providing support to aspects of the Trump 2.5 agenda.

Podcasts and Streamers

Donald Trump's 2024 presidential campaign was the first to aggressively target podcasts for voter engagement. These popular platforms with Gen Z remain relevant post-election and will be considered for inclusion in the White House briefing room.

- **Adin Ross**—A top-ranked streamer hosted Trump on his Kick stream as one of the early influencers who began to help mobilize the Gen Z male vote. During that interview, he gifted Trump a customized Cybertruck. Ross later attended the inauguration.

- **Andrew Schulz**—The stand-up comedian and podcaster hosted Trump on his show and immediately faced a backlash. Although he is mainly apolitical, he has hosted guests post-election to discuss Trump, especially radio host Charlamagne tha God.

- **Anna Khachiyan and Dasha Nekrasova**—The co-hosts of the *Red Scare* podcast have not interviewed Trump on the podcast but have intersected with personalities from the MAGA movement. They attended Keeperman's Coronation Ball during the inauguration. A tweet from RFK Jr. regarding Khachiyan and the comedian Tim Dillon was famously deleted.

- **Brett Cooper**—The top-ten podcaster left *The Daily Wire* at the end of 2024. Still, in her early 20s, she is arguably the most widely listened to conservative female personality online and has a growing base.

- **Jake and Logan Paul**—These brothers have separate brands and have some of the biggest audiences on YouTube and other streaming platforms. They have also diversified into entertainment streams and celebrity boxing. They engaged Trump separately during the 2024 election cycle and attended the inauguration festivities.

- **Joe Rogan**—The podcaster is also well-established in UFC circles. When Trump finally appeared on the *Joe Rogan Experience*, it quickly became one of the most-watched episodes ever. Notably, Kamala Harris did not appear. Over the last decade, Rogan has facilitated the growth of numerous independent platforms that have become prominent parts of the MAGA and MAHA movements.

- **John Shahidi**—The co-founder of the Shots Podcast Network was central to Trump's podcast engagement. Shots is the driving force behind the Full Send and Theo Von podcasts. Shahidi also helped register and mobilize voters ahead of the election. He advocates for continued engagement by the White House of podcasters and streamers parallel to mainstream media.
- **Jordan Peterson**—The Canadian psychologist and podcast host made waves in 2016 when he criticized political correctness. This led to a best-selling book and global tour. While he has worked closely with Elon Musk and Joe Rogan, he has often criticized Trump and the MAGA movement.
- **Kyle Forgeard**—The YouTuber is a lead Nelk Boys member who hosts the *Full Send Podcast*. They engaged President Trump in 2020 on Air Force One, and then he joined their podcast as a guest in 2022. They interviewed Trump again in 2024. Forgeard, who is Canadian, also spoke at campaign rallies in 2024. The Nelk Boys add a 'coolness' factor to the MAGA movement.
- **Konstantin Kisin**—The British-Russian co-host of the *Triggernometry* podcast would not be considered a 'bro' like the other podcasters listed here. He contributes to an intellectual undercurrent on the right that is anti-woke but Trump-adjacent. In a sense, he constitutes an offshoot of the atheist intellectualism of the 2010s.
- **Megyn Kelly**—The former Fox News host has become a successful podcaster. She is a go-to for the conservative movement and hosted Secretary Rubio for his first interview after being confirmed. While she had a famous dust-up in the presidential debates in 2016 with then-candidate Trump, she has since mended fences

with the president. She spoke at his last rally in Michigan the night before the election and, more recently, took a viral selfie with him at Super Bowl LIX.

- **Patrick Bet-David**—The founder of the Valuetainment platform emerged relatively recently as a force in digital media. In the lead-up to the election, he was a critical convenor of political figures on his platform and interviewed Donald Trump.
- **Piers Morgan**—The former newspaper editor and TV personality now hosts *Piers Morgan Uncensored* on *YouTube*. The show has become the meeting ground for the edgiest political debates online, with its clips routinely going viral. He is a friend of Trump and continues to advocate for the president on X and elsewhere.
- **Sage Steele**—The former ESPN anchor was allegedly removed from the network for her public stance on social and political issues. She has since emerged as a conservative voice online, launching a podcast through Bill Maher's studios. She is among the highest-profile African American women voices in the MAGA movement.
- **Shawn Ryan**—The former Navy Seal hosts a leading podcast on Spotify and has platformed a range of conservatives. He has a mix of political, military, and sports guests. He is close to a range of interlocuters in the conservative movement, including those in the new administration. He interviewed Trump in the lead-up to the 2024 election.
- **Sneako**—The trending streamer has often taken controversial positions, prompting his de-platforming across multiple sites. He praised Trump just before the election and is one of the most prolific influencers online, with a sizable youth following. After the election, he questioned the president's policies on Gaza.

- **Theo Von**—The comedian's podcast regularly ranks in the top 20 on U.S. podcast charts and has developed a following due to its edgy style. His pre-election interviews with Trump and Vance were crucial for reaching young males. After attending the inauguration, he spoke about the country coming together. He sees himself as a centrist.

There are more Democratic-aligned or center-left podcasts, examples being *Call Her Daddy* and *Pod Save America*. Still, whether the new Trump administration engages there is an open question. Another podcast, *The Breakfast Club*, was squarely in the Kamala Harris camp, but its hosts have commended some aspects of Trump's policies, for instance on social restoration.

Out There

Several individuals with followings are, while at times central, still on the fringe. They occasionally drive the political news cycle and have been nodes within the Trump or MAGA ecosystems.

- **Alex Jones**—The contrarian and conspiracist continues to be well-followed. In 2015, he interviewed Trump and has a close relationship with one-time Trump campaign advisor Roger Stone. While Jones is considered fringe due to his wild theories, he is close to Joe Rogan (both based in Austin) and has an extensive following.

- **Candace Owens**—The conservative activist had a falling out with *The Daily Wire* over policies on Israel. Since then, she has launched her podcast, *Candace*, which is regularly in the top five on Spotify. Her shows have delved into claims of Jewish influence and more far-flung topics, e.g., the gender of President Macron's wife.

- **Chris Brunet**—The former fellow at the Manhattan Institute is engaged in a sub-tweet movement railing against his former employer and has been accused of antisemitism. He confronts what he calls Zionist influence in conservative institutions, particularly those affiliated with billionaire Paul Singer. Paradoxically, he has also launched a sustained attack on Nick Fuentes's followers.

- **Laura Loomer**—The conservative activist practices shock journalism and has repeatedly tried to enter Trump's inner circle. In the Fall of 2024, after causing negative news stories, the Trump campaign moved to sideline her. Other surrogates, notably Congresswoman Marjorie Taylor Greene, also pushed back on her.

- **Liz Crokin**—Concentrating heavily on the Epstein/pedophilia nexus, Crokin's account ties the left and so-called establishment to conspiracy theories and scandals involving celebrities and trafficking rings. She has participated in events at Mar-a-Lago.

- **Milo**—The flamboyant conservative influencer from the United Kingdom re-emerged on X during the presidential election in 2024. He often gets into unique gossip fights with influential right-wing figures. He has managed crisis communications for Kanye West, also known as Ye.

- **Nick Fuentes**—Accused by the right of being 'a fed' and considered by most of being a fringe figure with extreme views, his followers are called groypers and are routinely accused of antisemitism. He was positive about Kamala Harris ahead of the election but mostly spent his time complaining about what he terms Zionist influence and echoing nativist themes.

Ultimately, the overall list of individuals in this chapter, across categories, serves as a repository of primary sources that can be turned to at any given time. New names will emerge relevant to the Trump 2.5 era. How observers curate information flows is another matter.

Staying current requires leveraging online platforms such as Spotify, Rumble, YouTube, or X.

Understanding the narrative beyond what is conveyed on mainstream news platforms is challenging. In addition, the fast-moving developments in the remainder of Trump's presidency will make it easy to lose track. Nothing is static.

V

THE WAY FORWARD

The fast and furious nature of the opening days and weeks of the Trump administration set off a domestic and global chain of events that will now take on a life of their own. This will generate both winners and losers. Moreover, there is a concerted effort to dislodge vested interests in the United States and globally irreversibly.

Some individuals, institutions, and countries will never regain what they lose in terms of positions and power. Others will feel suffocated by the new environment. As long as Trump is in the White House, a cross-section of America and the world will be in opposition, counting the days until 2029.

The volatility, however, also brings an unprecedented opening. The nature of America and the world order are being reshaped in a way not seen in decades. Entire sectors will be restructured, supply chains will reorient from end to end, and existing regulations will vanish overnight.

Regardless of political persuasion, the task for all will be to navigate the vicissitudes, mitigate the challenges, and capture opportunities as they arise.

Art of Possibility

During the first term, those who disapproved of President Trump's politics mobilized against him and his administration. This was successful in the short term, as he failed to win re-election. Others stayed out of the fray, which may have been wise, given the tumult that followed.

2025 is different. Trump 2.5 is different. The consolidated power now wielded by the Trump administration will lead to a completely different America and world, even if the MAGA-led Republican Party is defeated at the ballot box in 2028. The combination of domestic restructuring in America, adjacent to geopolitical and technological shifts, will give way to a different future.

This mindset of embracing the art of possibility will help those who seek it; builders, entrepreneurs, and creatives, especially, will find opportunity. This disposition will also ensure that one does not fall into the trap of the impossible. While engagement is the preferred path, certain stakeholders with a fundamental divergence in values and interests will choose disengagement as the only way forward.

As with all new governments and groups that take power, the biggest threat to the Trump 2.5 agenda is not opposition but the lack thereof. The effectiveness of the administration in the initial days and its consolidation of power will contribute to a sense of invincibility. That invariably fosters excess and in-group dynamics where only a purist form of alignment is acceptable. While the pendulum swung towards the Trump 2.5 era in the eyes of the public, it can always swing back.

Engagement

In pursuing engagement, understanding the areas with the highest potential for opportunity and developing a playbook will help achieve successful outcomes. This playbook should demonstrate an understanding of the focus areas

The Way Forward

at hand, zone of possibility at play, timeline, entry points within reach, and nature of approach.

Focus Areas

The Trump 2.5 agenda and actions thus far suggest five areas that offer the most potential: domestic manufacturing, natural resources, government spending, new technologies and cultural programs. Inherent volatility will also affect existing stakeholders, giving rise to opportunities for new entrants.

Manufacturing

The Trump administration will re-incentivize domestic manufacturing to try to reach levels not seen in decades. Putting aside the economic dynamics, there will be upside for domestic manufacturers. This will include reduced taxes, regulations, and barriers. A renewed mandate on 'buying American' in government procurement will also be a game changer.

The catalytic effect of this is still underestimated. There is still room for companies to have an early-mover advantage. Anything national security-related, especially upstream verticals, will be incentivized. While this would traditionally include the defense sector, today, it also encompasses artificial intelligence and everything related to processing power. Apple announced it would invest up to $500 billion in domestic investment and manufacturing in light of the current administration's policies.

Certain manufacturing policies introduced during Trump's first term were enhanced by President Biden and will be built upon; these will have more staying power. This included tariffs on China that affected key manufacturing sectors. On the other hand, the bipartisan CHIPS Act passed in 2022 that authorizes $50 billion in subsidies for the semiconductor industry is under threat. President Trump will instead look to secure the aluminum sector—critical to this industry—through tariffs as well as attract investments for the semiconductor industry through policy incentives, rather than grants.

Resources

Oil and gas are the centerpiece of the White House's natural resources strategy. The plan also encompasses critical minerals—specifically rare earth minerals—hydropower, biofuels, and nuclear energy, as outlined in an executive order that provided the direction. The domestic manufacturing focus and the reorientation of tax incentives may make many unprofitable projects profitable.

While the administration eschews the ESG rubric, it is not discarding new and renewable energy. Instead, it is shifting from wind and solar to other sources, as listed above. Funds already approved under the Inflation Reduction Act may be redirected to these areas. Openings will be missed if using only an ideological lens.

At the same time, nuclear development, mining ventures, and new oil and gas exploration can take years and decades to materialize. It is hard for a four-year administration to create opportunities in these areas. Careful evaluation on a per-project basis will be required.

Technology

Technology is integrated across sectors, but there are three categories where unique opportunities will emerge: crypto, artificial intelligence, and defense. The modernization of the weapons industry began over the past decade and was driven by stakeholders inside and outside the government. For example, one of the fastest-growing companies in recent years has been Anduril, which was founded in mid-2017. It is developing, among other things, new missile capabilities. The current administration's pursuit of an 'iron dome' will also require new defense technologies.

With an AI and crypto czar in the White House, these two domains will also present unique opportunities. In artificial intelligence, the announcement around Stargate AI received the most attention as an umbrella initiative for the industry. However, writ large, individuals or institutions helping to establish AI dominance for the United States will find incentives in the Trump 2.5 era. Even the Stargate AI announcement, which was unveiled with much fanfare, may see partners like Microsoft reduce their involvement over time.

While crypto has also been high on the agenda, speculative launches in the industry may undermine efforts. Recent meme coin launches have led to tremendous backlash, including from Argentina's president, Javier Milei. The Trump family's meme coin announcement also brought immense skepticism. Over the long term, benefits will flow most acutely to well-established cryptocurrencies, stablecoins, and the industry's essential infrastructure. The crypto reserve is another milestone that will shape how things unfold.

Government

The administration is looking to reduce the size of the government. This will involve executive-level decision-making and legislation by the Republican-led House. At the outset, this will lead to less of everything. At the same time, it will open the door to new talent and vendors with specific skills and capabilities.

This will be true for individuals and institutions specializing in data management and artificial intelligence. The principle of modernization across the government will also lead to upgrading equipment and infrastructure overseen by departments and agencies, such as defense and transportation.

Health is the area with the highest government spending, even beyond defense. The reorientation of HHS under RFK Jr. and the objective of chronic disease prevention will redirect funding to new research, therapies, and supply systems (in food). The bulk of mandatory spending falls under Medicaid, Medicare, and Social Security, which, at close to $2 trillion, accounts for nearly half of all federal spending. Any company that can help eliminate fraud, create efficiency gains, and provide preventative care that saves costs will find an audience.

Culture

The Trump administration is reducing ad hoc grants for cultural programs across agencies and departments. While total spending will be lower, the remaining spending will be reallocated. The Trump White House will reverse the past administration's agenda and promote social restoration.

The administration is looking to catalyze this cultural reorientation in America by restructuring the board and programming of the culturally centripetal Kennedy Center in this regard. This may open the door to new performers, new cultural institutions, and states that otherwise may have been excluded.

Society's boundaries for what is 'acceptable' will generally shift. As such, the zeitgeist may open to edgier cultural content that may have fallen under a stigma due to so-called cancel culture. New media platforms will have opportunities to cultivate new entertainment icons and encourage upstarts that overshadow existing celebrity culture.

Zone of Possibility

The potential for engagement can seem limited without a clear assessment of the underlying zone of possibility. This involves being clear about what opportunities can be pursued. Understanding the first-order mission as an individual and institution is the first step in this assessment.

This is easier said than done. In recent years, partly due to incorporating the private and non-profit sectors into a comprehensive agenda championed at forums such as Davos, it became challenging to disaggregate a company's mission from a transcendent societal mission. Typically, a lack of alignment with the agenda as broadly understood could lead to avoiding a partnership and any engagement altogether.

That can be problematic. A satellite launch company looks to launch satellites. A soup kitchen looks to feed the homeless. At an intrinsic level, there is a straightforward mandate on where engagement should be pursued. When doing so, this can lead to beneficial outcomes.

Take the example of global health organizations during the presidency of George W. Bush. While that administration was implacably against gay marriage and restricted gay rights, institutions seeking to combat HIV/AIDS, which has a higher incidence in gay communities, found an audience. The Bush administration enabled the most extensive health program by the U.S. government, the President's Emergency Plan for AIDS Relief. Thus, an expanded sense of the zone of possibility driven by a clear understanding of the mission-first orientation will enable the greatest opportunity.

Similarly, a rigorous view of the intrinsic red lines narrows the zone of possibility but in a straightforward and clear way. For example, a geospatial AI company may seek to work with the government, deploying its technology to improve all aspects of services, but still have a clear red line on the use of its technology for targeting weapons. Thus, it will avoid engaging the Department of Defense and intelligence agencies but still find ways to work with the government on efforts elsewhere.

Timeline

Given the fast-moving nature of developments, things will become urgent quickly. When USAID was under review early in the current administration, programs disappeared overnight. Finding a resolution within days meant the difference between surviving or not as a non-profit organization receiving funding. Conversely, opportunities will take time to materialize in areas where policies are not set. Rash investments may be prone to fail if not evaluated carefully.

Events and political developments will accelerate or decelerate the time horizon depending on how they impact stakeholders. For individuals and institutions aligned with the Trump 2.5 agenda, there is no time like the present because, by November 2026, the mid-term elections could end in—possibly—Democratic control of Congress and, thus, a political shift. Any number of world events could also divert and redirect the current agenda.

In engaging, it is important to consider the timeline beyond the Trump administration that aligns with deeper shifts that will last into the future. Once understood, bipartisan interests should guide thinking. For example, the tariffs on China enacted during the first Trump term remained during the Biden administration. On an ongoing basis, it will be essential to assess which policies and initiatives from the Trump 2.5 era will have staying power.

Reach

Stakeholders have varying levels of reach into the Trump administration and the associated MAGA movement. Understanding reach is a prerequisite to any engagement. Where are the entry points into the administration? Who is within existing networks or networks of networks connected to these entry points? Who else is knocking on their doors and competing for attention?

The best path for all is to go right to the top, to the president. Even Bill Gates, who has been the subject of criticism within MAGA movement, had a three-hour dinner with Trump before his inauguration, with just the two of them and their respective chiefs of staff present. Trump can override any part of the Trump 2.5 agenda if it is politically expedient.

The preceding chapter provides a universe of entry points. In a democratized digital landscape, such as on X, anyone can engage and be engaged. The fact that the Department of Government Efficiency is named after a meme coin that started as a joke shows the spectacular nature of the flat online world. This is slightly worrying, but it signifies that the entry points are there for all.

A structured understanding will help inform how best to engage. In addition to existing relationships, new ones can be cultivated, but it will require traditional and non-traditional means. The Trump administration has displaced regular stalwarts across departments. While lobbyists can be hired, it will cause challenges if stakeholders within the MAGA movement are not onside.

Approach

Each individual, investor, institution, and country should have a tailored approach. Relevant stakeholders across the board will need to ensure that it is consistently updated. There is no one-size-fits-all approach. Depending on the scope, a team with sufficient funding would need to be in place.

Individuals

Everyday individuals are in both the best and worst positions. Most events in the Trump 2.5 era will be beyond the control of any individual in America and around the world. It may not seem this way when consuming news and perusing social media. Everyone appears to be part of the conversation.

The Trump 2.5 era will bring openings and opportunities, but it is up to individuals to find them. It is useful to monitor developments closely. For example, while the Trump administration has announced assistance for IVF, how, where, and when can it be accessed? Similarly, stemming the flow of illegal migrants could lower housing prices in select urban rental markets but determining where in particular will require more in-depth tracking. There are other follow-on effects to be aware of.

This is the administration for the next four years and its policies will shape all aspects of society and the economy. Individuals, especially those heading households, will need to learn to navigate it successfully. What was once dependable is no longer.

Investors

In times of volatility, there is a tremendous upside for investors. However, there is also a downside for investors caught in sudden swings and manipulated markets. With the convergence of the crypto industry with parts of the MAGA movement and its Gen Z base, there is potential for 'rug pulls,' whereby a crypto project is announced with much fanfare to a mass audience, and inside investors quickly sell at a high.

Markets will continue to move quickly with the rapid flow of information. For instance, at the outset of the administration, Chinese company DeepSeek launched a new AI model that depended on less compute power. NVIDIA, the leading global company providing computing power, saw its stock price decline by 20% almost overnight. However, it made back most of those losses over the next month and then declined again.

The volatility in leading equities signals investors should instead turn to where value will build over time. Due to rapidly changing policies and politics, the vicissitudes of the Trump 2.5 era will catch investors off-guard if they play positions for short-term gain. The best approach is to determine the priorities of the Trump 2.5 agenda based on this primer and then make long-term bets on undervalued assets and equities in correlated areas.

Institutions

Most large institutions, as well as smaller enterprises, have developed an engagement approach for the Trump 2.5 era. However, many are still taken aback by the pace of change. Organizations receiving federal funding were caught flat-footed early on. Adapting will not be easy, but it is possible.

The first steps are to identify relevant focus areas and define a zone of possibility. Institutions must then navigate the situation carefully. Being mission-first does not mean jumping from one political side to the other. Leading in a time of polarization requires adeptness and empathy.

Within the Trump movement, there is an economic populist wing. The American population on the left and right routinely identify corporate greed as problematic. Leading companies will need to find ways to not just profit-seek but also partner with the new administration on urban renewal, building the domestic manufacturing base, and revitalizing American infrastructure. This will help protect the narrative for corporations that pursue engagement.

Executives at institutions will also want to put in place three elements: outreach capabilities, a monitoring unit, and a nomenclature audit. The previous chapters serve as a resource, but each institution should dive deep into the constellation of its areas of concern. To illustrate, renewable energy companies should endeavor to understand the North Dakota political environment in detail, given Interior Secretary Doug Burgum's background there. In addition, who are the go-betweens between Burgum and Energy Secretary Chris Wright? Further afield, who are the identified individuals from the American First Policy Institute, influential in the Trump 2.5 era, who worked on energy policy?

The extent to which most leading institutions understand the latest news through mainstream sources is still surprising. If it does not already exist, a monitoring unit should be set up to track developments, leveraging digital publications and online voices that directly understand the Trump 2.5 agenda. This monitoring should happen objectively and not through a partisan filter.

Finally, and this is relevant for institutions with global reach, a thorough nomenclature audit is essential. Over the last decade and a half, a fine-tuned nomenclature and set of acronyms have taken hold. From 'Build Back Better' to 'diversity, equity, inclusion' to 'environment, social, governance,' well-used terms are now politicized, if not antiquated. Deploying a non-nomenclature style is the best way forward.

Countries

Almost all countries have developed strategies for dealing with the current Trump administration, especially those directly affected by American moves, such as tariffs. More generally, a deep policy apparatus exists for relations with America. None of this is good enough for the Trump 2.5 era.

During the first Trump term, countries took three principal approaches: responsiveness, resistance, or alliance building. The first Trump administration came and went, and most bilateral engagement was centered on achieving quick policy wins through haphazard actions. Others funded an alternative ecosystem globally, and once the Biden administration returned, so did many discarded policies.

This Trump administration is different, and the changes it precipitates will be lasting. Moreover, there is a deeper consolidation of the government bureaucracy on the one hand and the political apparatus of the Republican Party on the other by the president's team. Relying on past channels and back-channels will be less effective and could backfire. To avoid this, countries seeking to engage the United States during this period should take a tailored approach to

The Way Forward

Trump 2.5 beyond their existing policy structures, comprising a purposely built inter-departmental team, dedicated resources, and a reorientation of language.

Due to wholesale changes arising from Trump 2.5, the cross-functional team needs to comprise representatives across a government's apparatus. The United States under President Trump is shifting the nature of the global geopolitical and economic system. New alliance formation will be required. Enforcing existing international norms will become, at times, impossible, and new mechanisms will need to be developed vis-à-vis the U.S. in concert with other countries.

This team will also need to enable new relationship building in the U.S. Most foreign policy engagement by countries is predicated on relationships within regular meeting grounds, think tanks, and traditional media. This reinforces not just biases but also narrows influence in the Trump ecosystem. For instance, is there a dedicated diplomat based in Palm Beach? It is self-evident that a country with a dedicated consulate next to Mar-a-Lago would be effective with the MAGA movement. Almost none have taken this step.

A successful approach will require adequate resources. Funding enables an improved online presence, such as engaging with podcasts and streaming platforms. It also can support events that have rising importance, such as those related to space exploration and America's 250th anniversary. Extensive financial resources will be needed for large-scale investment into America. The sovereign wealth funds in the Gulf will take the lead in this, but all countries should consider this; even Italy has a sovereign wealth fund. Sovereign instruments have the capability to help lead the private sector with well-placed investments in America.

Finally, countries have been accustomed to specific language over the past three decades pertaining to a rules-based order that was already fading and is definitively shifting with the Trump 2.5 era. Reorienting this language is fundamental to engaging with the Trump administration.

Disengagement

Many Americans disagree with the Trump 2.5 agenda. Around the world, many people and countries are aghast at America's direction, which has effectively dismantled conventional approaches and institutions. In liberal circles, Trump, the MAGA movement, and the new Trump administration represent existential threats to America, democracy, and core values. For this group, there is only one choice in the Trump 2.5 era: disengagement.

The intention would be to develop an alternative to the current administration and ultimately bide time until a transition. Certain institutions, countries, and leading individuals would want to achieve this. However, doing so is much more difficult this time around. This is not 2017 or 2021. As this primer has covered, there is a very different feel to 2025 and the Trump 2.5 era.

Setting aside the dynamics of President Trump, the administration, and the MAGA movement, which have already been covered, the Democratic Party and its institutional elite are in disarray. While the first Trump term provided a brief interruption, that coalition has effectively controlled the levers of power since 2009 and Barack Obama's rise to the presidency. Today, they are older, less responsive, and integrated with an array of special interests.

This is a regular pattern in American political life: An insurgent political force is able to dislodge an incumbent one that has held power for some time. Accordingly, the Democratic Party will need to acknowledge that its popularity and resonance are declining as the American public seeks change. Messages of restoration by the same politicians of the past will not be effective.

That being said, a strategy that leads to regrouping, mobilizing new resources, and delivering results could serve as a counterweight to the Trump 2.5 era. If disengagement is the preferred path, this is the only way forward.

Regrouping

Regrouping must start with admitting that something went wrong and that staying the course is not possible. Internationally, it would mean accepting certain narratives. How the wars in Ukraine and Gaza escalated was an abdication of American leadership. The relationship with China undermined American manufacturers and workers for decades. The nature of the existing rules-based order is not sustainable.

Domestically, similar *mea culpas* are needed. The maximalist policies on social issues reached a breaking point for many Americans, even among the Democratic Party's traditional base. The party did not sufficiently acknowledge the responsibility of past Democratic administrations for inflation and illegal migration. Without a full reckoning on domestic and foreign policy, there is no basis for moving forward.

The second part of regrouping is leadership. Within the Republican Party, close to Trump are leaders like Tulsi Gabbard, RFK Jr., Elon Musk, and JD Vance, the third-youngest vice president in American history. Together, they are tossing out taboos and engaging with new cultural forces.

The general public sees a Democratic Party led by past Presidents Joe Biden and Barack Obama, former Secretary of State Hillary Clinton, former Speaker Nancy Pelosi, Senate Minority Leader Chuck Schumer, and perhaps former Vice President Kamala Harris. While a cosmetic regrouping might be preferred, without grassroots enthusiasm it will not resonate. This regrouping of leadership must be matched by a renewed agenda that considers the sentiments of most

Americans and their frustrations of the last 16 years, primarily under Democratic leadership.

This regrouping is not a lost cause. There are voters who will not vote for the Trump 2.5 agenda for entrenched ideological reasons. Special interests within the MAGA coalition may drive policies against popular sentiment. Yet, without regrouping, the Democratic Party will be stuck pointing out problems instead of presenting solutions and an alternative.

Resources

In addition to regrouping, new resources will be required. This Trump administration has been effective in its early days in dismantling the public funding apparatus for institutions linked to partisans aligned with Democratic Party positions, ranging from universities to non-profit organizations to media institutions. Collectively, these institutions have amplified Democratic messaging and even mobilized voters across the years.

In the Trump 2.5 era, these forces will not have the same public purse to rely on. The institutional fabric of those who see themselves in opposition will need to recalibrate. This is not at all impossible. While there are significant donors on the GOP side, as outlined in the last chapter, there is an equal, if not higher, number on the Democratic side. Even more so, there are interests that would support pushing back on the Trump 2.5 agenda. This includes philanthropists who have far-reaching funding networks. The challenge is to convince these existing funding networks to finance narratives and institutions that may undermine their interests due to the economic policies being advanced.

Results

A disengagement approach will succeed only if it produces demonstrable results. For President Trump, the results of his first term before the pandemic ultimately resonated with voters, who contrasted it with the Biden administration. This was most apparent in economic issues, inflation, and immigration. While the Democratic Party is out of power at the federal level, 23 states have Democratic governors. In addition, America's three largest cities, Chicago, New York, and Los Angeles, have Democratic mayors.

If, over the next two years, a consolidated coalition of stakeholders, political and otherwise, brings together philanthropists, the private sector, and non-profits to showcase a counter-model of success in these states and cities, it will resonate with voters. This would present a problem for the Trump 2.5 agenda, but this is a big if.

In the initial days the approach appears to mirror the same inclinations from the Democratic Party during the first Trump term: resistance, not results. Moreover, in America's three largest cities, led by the Democratic Party, the reality undermines the narrative. In New York, the mayor's office has been immersed in turmoil. In Chicago, the mayor has an approval rating in the low teens. In Los Angeles, the mayor has faced consternation from residents after the wildfires.

In Excess

In the current scenario, the Trump 2.5 agenda is ascendant. It is a force to be reckoned with for America and the world. Yet, the Trump administration may overestimate its political mandate.

The speed of this Trump administration may be its biggest curse. It has quickly assumed incumbency of power, which implies that it will also be blamed when things go wrong. Without room for dissent within MAGA circles, this could lead to blind spots and contribute to poorly-thought-out policy. When that brings about challenges or crises, there will be no one to blame but President Trump and his team.

In addition, a fair number of changes will drastically affect livelihoods, especially via jobs lost due to cuts in federal funding. While a portion of funding recipients are political, most employees losing their jobs are everyday Americans with no political involvement. A lack of empathy amidst all these changes could create political headwinds.

While this administration has tighter messaging than the first Trump term, the same cannot be said for its supporters on social media. With a free-flowing environment on X, multiple accounts that have large followings and claim to represent the MAGA movement amplify racist, sexist, homophobic, and xenophobic language.

These voices are conceivably not at the core of the White House. Vice President Vance has an interracial family. Treasury Secretary Scott Bessent is the highest-ranking U.S. openly gay official in history. Susie Wiles is the first-ever female chief of staff and arguably the second most powerful person in the administration. On issues and policies, Trump and his team attempt to characterize positions as deriving from an America First philosophy and not any underlying 'isms.'

Ultimately, this will be a battle of narratives, and as administration officials amplify accounts that indulge in more extreme positions, it could become an increasing problem. The tendency within the Trump ecosystem is to accuse the media of bias. There is also a general aversion to policing language. The Trump 2.5 agenda is that much more vulnerable because it is predisposed to dismiss valid criticism of positions that cross the line within its own ranks.

Another challenge will be the valid public perception that billionaires control decision-making in this Trump administration. Over a dozen billionaires have been appointed to key government positions. With emphases on AI, technology, and economic growth, broader socioeconomic trendlines may be ignored. Criticism has already emerged within the MAGA movement regarding the outsized role of technologists in the administration.

Overall, there is limited room to maneuver. It is unlikely that there will be a sustained push for bipartisanship or compromise from all sides over the next 12 months. There will also be rising confrontations with the judicial branch. Any excesses by the administration will probably be indulged rather than scaled back. As always, it will come down to outcomes. If, by the midterms, there is demonstrable progress on government efficiency, economic growth, global conflicts, and immigration, that will overshadow much of the overreach undertaken to achieve it.

Mars-Shot

Political debates, while important, overshadow other impactful developments underway. It has been considerable time since a single event captured the collective imagination and pushed the boundaries of innovation. Politically, the fall of the Berlin Wall would be one such moment. Outside of politics, finding another example in recent years is hard. Arguably, it was the Space Race that last did that.

This is what makes a potential Mars-shot—like the moonshot of the 1960s—so potent. What this could unlock regarding the bounds of human imagination is unknown.

In the coming term, this Mars-shot will be the goal. In 1962, then-President John F. Kennedy gave a landmark speech, "We choose to go to the Moon," in which he reinforced that America would reach the Moon during that decade. By the time this was achieved, he had passed, but the milestone stood the test of time. The Trump administration will promote space exploration during this term, with Elon Musk already playing a centripetal role.

In advance of the inauguration, Trump, as president-elect, hosted a dinner with Jeff Bezos, who founded the private spaceflight company Blue Origin. Musk, who has been a rival of Bezos, joined the dinner. Although they represent a united front, for now, this might change. In addition, the present executive orders and budget cuts also mean that NASA is being reviewed. This could slow progress and agility in the months ahead.

That said, the appointment of a forward-looking NASA chief and the administration's disposition in favor of space travel, a Mars-shot, will be in the cards during the second Trump term. Approximately every two years, an alignment between Earth and Mars creates a launch window. The next window is towards the end of 2026. Traveling to Mars would likely take six to nine months, although this depends on a number of factors.

Whether SpaceX will be ready to send its Starship vehicle by then is an open question, but that is the plan. The uncrewed mission would be a key step ahead of a potential human spaceflight to the red planet. No other companies or countries have viable spacecraft that could reach the surface of Mars.

The second launch window for Mars will be in the final weeks of the administration. Thus, if everything were going according to plan, there would be a crewed mission launching to Mars then, which would be revolutionary. However, most probably, humanity will not reach Mars until after Trump leaves office, which will be further into the future, towards 2040. Nevertheless, this effort could bring together unprecedented innovation and a collective spirit of exploration. Space exploration is much more inspiring than building a giant data center or producing a more eloquent chatbot, which is where artificial intelligence is settling, at least in most people's eyes.

250th Anniversary

One of the initial executive orders President Trump signed was "Celebrating America's 250th Birthday." During the

The Way Forward 175

campaign, Trump suggested a year-long celebration starting in May 2025, after Memorial Day. It is not yet decided when the commemoration of the landmark event will start, but it will undoubtedly last for months and culminate with a celebration on July 4th, 2026, marking the anniversary of America's founding and Declaration of Independence.

The effort will be to create an affair that is inclusive and unifying. However, in today's partisan age, there is likely to be politicization by all sides and controversies emerging in the media. Decisions about which narratives and individuals to highlight will be debated. For instance, the administration intends to create a National Garden of American Heroes for the anniversary. Who will be featured there, and will it be acceptable across the political divide?

Regardless, the 250th anniversary promises to be a spectacle and a mobilizing moment for American industry and innovators. With Trump's background as a showman and entertainer, he will see this as an iconic moment. The spectacle will not be limited to one day or one location. It will be replicated across almost all 50 states for some time.

Contrasted with the first term, corporations have lined up to engage with the new administration and participate in full force in these celebrations. Thus, it is expected that there will be moments similar to those of the World's Fair of years past, with a spotlight on both the American past and its technological future. There will be associated competitions and showcases. An administration task force is still developing formal announcements related to this.

Skeptics tend to deride such events and the basis behind them. Indeed, for those with severe disagreements with the Trump 2.5 agenda, pursuing an approach of disengagement will extend to the 250th anniversary. Yet, those who embrace the moment will have a sense of unbridled momentum. There will be a political embrace for projects announced during this anniversary period, probably more so in Republican-led states. This is also the ultimate moment for the art of possibility.

Beyond Trump

The current moment centers on President Donald J. Trump and will last for the next four years. At the same time, the Trump 2.5 era will pass, and by January 20, 2029, another president will be in the White House. As always, events—even seismic political ones—come and go. It is instructive to understand the current moment and examine how it will contribute to a new opening and related shifts that will define the next 15 years and beyond.

This primer has attempted to understand Trump from within his perspective and that of his supporters, who constitute the plurality of the United States of America. There is a tendency to base reactions—even to this primer—on instinctive feelings about Donald Trump. This may be unavoidable, but it is to the detriment of navigating the way forward.

The pace of developments will be unsettling, if not overwhelming. In that sense, things are beyond the grasp, control, and influence of any single individual. The dispassionate analysis is intended to meet the moment for what it is and help those who desire it craft the best possible path to success for their interests and agenda.

Nothing is set, and the future is yours to shape.

ADDITIONAL RESOURCES

There are innumerable resources on American politics. A variety of sources is listed to enable access to information so readers can independently weigh what is accurate, but their inclusion does not represent an endorsement. All must survey a range of literature and adjust accordingly. The official website for the book, TrumpPrimer.com, will have more details on accessing resources.

Books

Most long-form publications analyzing Donald J. Trump and the politics surrounding him have a built-in bias. Below are books by President Trump and his family that provide a primary source point of view. In addition, several publications are listed by leading figures in the Make America Great Again movement. Other perspectives are included from observers, some of which may seem like opposition tracts. It is up to the reader to determine how to situate and discern the best approximation of truth.

The Trump family

- *The Art of the Deal* (1987)—Donald J. Trump
- *The Art of the Comeback* (1997)—Donald J. Trump

- *The America We Deserve* (2000) — Donald J. Trump
- *Time to Get Tough: Making America #1 Again* (2011) — Donald J. Trump
- *Crippled America: How to Make America Great Again* (2015) — Donald J. Trump
- *Triggered: How the Left Thrives on Hate and Wants to Silence Us* (2019) — Donald Trump Jr.
- *Breaking History: A White House Memoir* (2022) — Jared Kushner
- *All in the Family: The Trumps and How We Got This Way* (2024) — Fred C. Trump III
- *Melania* (2024) — Melania Trump

The MAGA+ perspective

- *Hillbilly Elegy: A Memoir of a Family and Culture in Crisis* (2016) — JD Vance
- *The Case for Trump* (2019) — Victor Hanson
- *The Real Anthony Fauci: Bill Gates, Big Pharma, and the Global War on Democracy and Public Health* (2021) — Robert F. Kennedy Jr.
- *Rigged: How the Media, Big Tech, and the Democrats Seized Our Elections* (2022) — Mollie Hemingway
- *Taking Back Trump's America: Why We Lost the White House and How We'll Win It Back* (2022) — Peter Navarro

Observations and Opposition

- *American Carnage: On the Front Lines of the Republican Civil War and the Rise of President Trump* (2020) — Tim Alberta
- *A Very Stable Genius: Donald J. Trump's Testing of America* (2020) — Philip Rucker

Additional Resources

- *January 6th Report* (2022) — The January 6 Select Committee
- *The Presidency of Donald J. Trump: A First Historical Assessment* (2022) — Julian E. Zelizer
- *The Trump Indictments: The 91 Criminal Counts Against the Former President of the United States* (2023) — Ali Velshi
- *The Trump Tapes* (2023) — Bob Woodward
- *All or Nothing: How Trump Recaptured America* (2025) — Michael Wolff

News

To get the latest developments in real time and unfiltered, it is best to aggregate an account on X following the names listed in the third chapter, "People & Positions." In addition, the account @RapidResponse47 is the White House's principal communications channel for conveying its narrative. What follows is a list of platforms that curate relatively apolitical daily news and long-form magazines that provide political perspectives and analysis that can shed light on the Trump 2.5 era.

Daily Reads

- *Axios* (axios.com) — Digital platform that provides quick insights
- *Politico* (politico.com) — News focused on American politics
- *Semafor* (semafor.com) — Business-oriented publication that has neutral tone
- *The Hill* (thehill.com) — Coverage of happenings in Congress

- *The Washington Post* (washingtonpost.com) — Newspaper of record in the nation's capital

Longer Analysis

- *City Journal* (city-journal.org) — Platform with conservative analysis of social issues
- *Compact* (compactmag.com) — Online magazine that critiques modern liberalism
- *The American Conservative* (theamericanconservative.com) — Populist conservative perspective
- *The Atlantic* (theatlantic.com) — Long-form features on modern America
- *The Bulwark* (thebulwark.com) — Refuge for the Never Trump movement

Overviews & Context

Many online sites have useful databases of relevant information, with some more historical and others current. These are listed here, alongside some longer-form documents that provide a deeper understanding of President Trump and the Trump 2.5 era.

- America First Policy Institute (americafirstpolicy.com/issues) — Briefs across policy areas from the think tank linked to the MAGA movement
- Department of Government Efficiency (doge.gov) — Ongoing tracker of every program being terminated by DOGE efforts
- Donald Trump 2024 *Time* Person of the Year (time.com/person-of-the-year-2024-donald-trump) — Interview with President Trump just prior to the second term
- Open Secrets (opensecrets.org) — Searchable database of all political contributions by donor or politician

Additional Resources

- Political Appointee Tracker (ourpublicservice.org/performance-measures/political-appointee-tracker/) — Index of top positions requiring senate confirmation
- Project 2025 (project2025.org) — Comprehensive playbook put together by leading conservatives ahead of 2024 elections
- Republican Party Platform for 2024 (rncplatform.donaldjtrump.com) — The official platform that Donald Trump ran on in the elections
- Rollcall Trump Speeches Archive (rollcall.com/factbase/trump/search) — A unique index of speeches and interviews over the years
- "The Empire and Ego of Donald Trump" (nytimes.com/1983/08/07/business/the-empire-and-ego-of-donald-trump.html) — A very early article covering the initial rise of Donald Trump
- Trump Organization (trump.com) — The website for the Trump family business with a listing of holdings

**Everything happens gradually,
then suddenly**

ABOUT THE AUTHOR

Strategist, investor, and writer Taufiq Rahim focuses on the intersection of geopolitics and technology in a changing world. He began his career in Washington, DC, and is currently building platforms within the 2040 nexus.

Over the last two decades and across five continents, Rahim has driven investment, convened conversations, and forged partnerships to address critical issues such as economic growth, political transition, and global poverty. He is often cited by the *Financial Times, Washington Post, New York Times, Bloomberg, CNN, CNBC, Al Jazeera, Arab News*, and more. He is the author of *Middle East in Crisis & Conflict: A Primer*.

Rahim is originally from Vancouver, Canada, and resides in New York. When not writing, he finds himself equally at home in the sweltering sands of the desert or the fresh powder on the mountain.

www.ingramcontent.com/pod-product-compliance
Lightning Source LLC
Chambersburg PA
CBHW020542030426
42337CB00013B/942